W9-BWW-309

A COUNTRY MUSIC CHRISTMAS

CHRISTMAS SONGS, MEMORIES, FAMILY PHOTOGRAPHS AND RECIPES
FROM AMERICA'S FAVORITE COUNTRY AND GOSPEL STARS

EDIE HAND & BUDDY KILLEN

BROADWAY BOOKS
NEW YORK

PUBLISHED BY BROADWAY BOOKS

Copyright © 2006 by Edie Hand and Buddy Killen

All Rights Reserved

Published in the United States by Broadway Books, an imprint of The Doubleday Broadway Publishing Group, a division of Random House, Inc., New York. www.broadwaybooks.com

BROADWAY BOOKS and its logo, a letter B bisected on the diagonal, are trademarks of Random House, Inc.

Book design by rlf design

Library of Congress Cataloging-in-Publication Data
Hand, Edie, 1951–
    A country music Christmas : Christmas songs, memories, family photographs and recipes from America's favorite country and gospel stars / Edie Hand and Buddy Killen.
        p.   cm.
    Includes index.
    1. Christmas cookery. 2. Country musicians—Anecdotes. I. Killen, Buddy. II. Title.

TX739.2.C45H356   2006
641.5'686—dc22
                                                    2006042514

ISBN-13: 978-0-7679-2316-3
ISBN-10: 0-7679-2316-2

Printed in Japan

10 9 8 7 6 5 4 3 2 1

First Edition

To Edie's brothers,

the late David, Terry, and Phillip Blackburn,

who all loved riding horses with her

at dawn on Christmas.

Contents

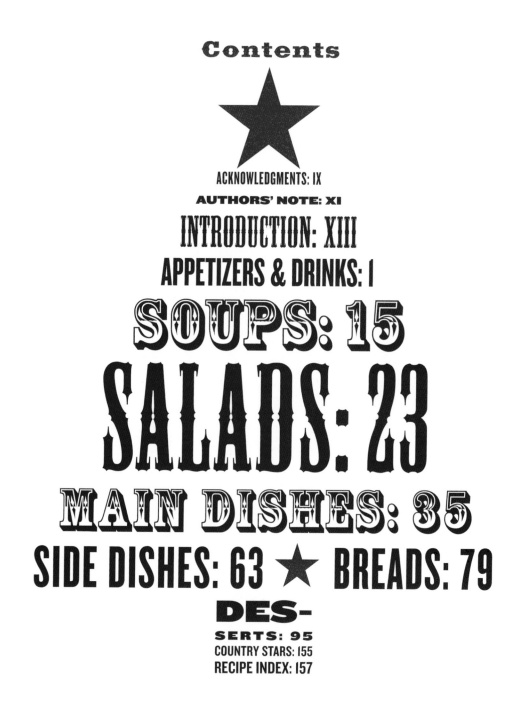

Acknowledgments

OUR GOAL in compiling this book was to provide country and gospel music fans with heartwarming stories, delectable family recipes, rarely seen photos, and amazing music from their favorite artists. We have been blessed to have had so many friends and family members helping us see this project to completion. There is simply no way we could have done without them. We want to extend our deepest heartfelt thanks to each of them. We are grateful to this wonderful team of special individuals: Jennifer Josephy, our editor; Harvey Klinger, our literary agent; Kathy Goodwin, Edie's personal assistant; Megan Pool, Buddy Killen's personal assistant; The Visibility Company and Bob Layne; Mark Aldridge; Georgia Blagovich; John Clore; Keith Dunn; Brian Edwards; Karen M. Fleming; the Country Music Hall of Fame and Museum; Kimberly Ford; Kristen Green; Pam Hyatt; Kat Korac; Bobbi Jo Lathan; Carolyn Killen; Cathy Nakos; Judy Spencer Nelon; Marlene Palmer; Jackie Proffit and Teri Watson of St. Jude/Country Cares in Nashville; Heidi Raphael; Michael Sutton; Kirt Webster and the staff of Webster and Associates; Viking and the chefs from Viking Culinary Arts Center in Atlanta, Georgia; Quito McKenna and Josh Doepke, in charge of testing all the recipes; chefs Melissa Akins, Betsy Battenhouse, Jill Davis, Kathy Foster, Paul Greever, and Gwen Grant; Larry Hall, musical arranger; and Andy Kern, engineer. A special thank-you to Joe Meador, Grand Entertainment; Jerry Bridges, Night Town Music; and Randy Campbell of Making Strides at the Children's Hospital of Alabama.

Authors' Note

WE HAVE PLEDGED 10 percent of the royalties received from the sale of the book to the Country Music Hall of Fame and Museum in Nashville, Tennessee; 10 percent of the royalties to St. Jude Children's Research Hospital in Memphis, Tennessee; and 10 percent of the royalties to the Edie Hand Foundation in Birmingham, Alabama.

Country music and Southern gospel music are woven into our history. Music has been so important to us, and we will always be grateful for the opportunities it has given us. We are grateful to the Country Music Hall of Fame and Museum for the work it does to preserve and celebrate this tradition. Visit them at www.countrymusic halloffame.com.

St. Jude Children's Research Hospital is unlike any other pediatric treatment and research facility in many important ways. The discoveries made at St. Jude have changed how the world treats children with cancer and other catastrophic diseases. As a world-renowned research hospital, St. Jude is where doctors across the globe send their toughest cases and most vulnerable patients. And at St. Jude, no one pays for treatment beyond what is covered by insurance, and those without insurance are never asked to pay. It is an inspiring organization that we are privileged to support. See www.stjude.org for more on the organization.

The Edie Hand Foundation's mission is to raise and donate money to Alabama communities and national charities. Our hope is to provide caregivers with funds to help raise a child or to defeat an incurable disease or to provide children with joy at Christmas. The Edie Hand Foundation supports groups like Making Strides at Children's Hospital of Alabama for kids and young adults with motor dysfunctions like Edie's brother, the late Terry Blackburn, and children like Allie and Mattie Templeton. See www.makingstrides.org for more details on how little steps can one day add up to the big steps that a full, independent life has to offer. In addition, this year the Edie Hand Foundation will "Share the Art of Giving" with the Christmas Spirit Foundation, which focuses on enhancing Christmas Spirit through programs for children, families, and the environment. Visit their Web site, www.christmasspiritfoundation.org. Also see www.ediehandfoundation.org.

Introduction

THE IDEA FOR THIS BOOK came about one day as the two of us sat reminiscing about what Christmas was like when we were children. We spoke of how excited we were on Christmas morning, opening the packages that were mysteriously left by a man in a red suit with a long white beard. We never saw him, but we knew he had been there. Although we wondered how he got into our houses because neither of us had a chimney, when you're young, you don't question Santa Claus. Then, after opening our gifts, we looked forward to the wonderful feasts that had been prepared by our mothers. We thought of the scrumptious dishes made from recipes that had been handed down through generations; mouthwatering, deliciously prepared chicken and ham, potatoes and gravy, and biscuits that would melt in your mouth. After that came the desserts. We remember the banana pudding, peach and apple turnovers, and all types of cakes—chocolate, orange, lemon, and, the greatest of all, coconut cake made with freshly grated coconut and the milk straight from the shell.

As we struggled to get past our hunger pangs, we turned our conversation to the songs we always loved to hear at Christmas—the old songs like "O Come All Ye Faithful," "White Christmas," and "Jingle Bells" or maybe one of the new songs introduced that year.

We realized that everyone has a special Christmas memory and many have a song or a special recipe or two they might enjoy sharing. And what would be more fun than putting together a book containing seasonal memories, special songs, and recipes from some of our favorite celebrities? So off we went and called what seemed like everyone we knew to see who wanted to help.

The support we received was overwhelming! The quick responses from virtually everyone we asked to participate in this project were extraordinarily gratifying. We're sorry that, in the end, we couldn't squeeze all of the contributors into this book, so we hope we'll be able to do another someday soon. We are so grateful to everyone who was willing to help us make *A Country Music Christmas* possible. It is in their names that we have pledged a large percentage of the profits from this book to the Country Music Hall of Fame and Museum in Nashville, Tennessee; the Edie Hand Foundation in Birmingham, Alabama; and St. Jude Children's Research Hospital in Memphis, Tennessee.

We hope that you will enjoy this book for many years to come and that each and every year you will open up the book and put on the CD of holiday music we have produced for everyone who loves Christmas as much as we do.

Edie Hand

Buddy Killen

APPE-
TIZERS &
DRINKS
APPETIZERS
& DRINKS ★ APPETIZERS & DRINKS ★ APPETIZERS & DRINKS
APPE-
TIZERS
& DRINKS

Jim Ed Brown

IM ED BROWN is no stranger to the top of the charts. Beginning his recording career with his sisters, Maxine and Bonnie, in 1956, Jim Ed had such hits as "Three Bells" and "Little Jimmy Brown," which were country-pop crossover hits for the group. Jim Ed began recording solo projects in 1965 and had numerous country hits. In 1976, he teamed up with Helen Cornelius to record a long string of duet hits. The two were recognized in 1977 with the Vocal Duo of the Year award. Remembered as the host of Nashville's *You Can Be a Star* television show, he continues to be an active member of the *Grand Ole Opry.*

HOLIDAYS BRING BACK wonderful memories of my dear sweet mama. I can just imagine her right now in the kitchen cooking with a pinch of this and a dab of that. She was always experimenting with recipes and putting together meals with loving care. Mama taught me how to cook before I went into the army. Her lessons have served me well.

Christmas is a time for sharing a piece of you with your family and friends. I do just that, by baking up some old-fashioned recipes for folks I like. But I do it Mama's way. I like to think she's in the kitchen with me. It sure does bring a medley of songs out of me on Christmas Day.

I recommend that you bake and break some bread with someone you love this Christmas . . . and for all of the Christmases to come.

Pop-a-Top Friendship Cup

Mama taught me how to cook and how to share my cookin'. Add this recipe to your list of holiday appetizers, and watch your family and friends smile. Makes 4 quarts

    2 cups sliced, peeled apples
    2 cups sliced, peeled pears
    2 cups quartered peaches (about 3 medium)
    2 cups raisins, optional
    5 cups firmly packed light brown sugar
    5 cups granulated sugar
    1 cinnamon stick
    1 quart brandy

1. Combine the apples, pears, peaches, raisins (if using), sugars, and cinnamon stick in a large bowl. Gently toss to mix. Let the fruit stand for 1 hour, gently tossing (use your fingers to avoid bruising the fruit) every 15 minutes. Remove the cinnamon stick.

2. Transfer the fruit mixture to a $1^1/_2$-gallon stone crock with a seal. Add the brandy and gently stir to mix. Place the seal on the crock and let it stand in a cool dark place for 6 months. As you enjoy the mixture, feel free to replace the amount of sugared fruits and brandy that you remove with an equal portion of fresh fruit, sugar, and brandy.

Jessi Colter-Jennings

$\mathcal{P}$ERHAPS BEST KNOWN as the wife of the late Waylon Jennings, Jessi Colter was the only significant female singer-songwriter to emerge from the mid-1970s "outlaw" movement. As a teenager she left her hometown of Phoenix, Arizona, to tour with Duane Eddie. Jessi has written songs for some of music's greats, including Don Gibson, Dottie West, and Nancy Sinatra. In 1975, Jessi broke through with one of her own songs, "I'm Not Lisa," a single from her LP *I'm Jessi Colter,* which reached the number one spot on *Billboard*'s country chart, while making the top five on the pop charts. Before Waylon's death in 2002, the couple moved back to Phoenix, where Jessi still lives.

CHRISTMAS at the Jennings's house was such a grand affair. Waylon and I always had a beautiful twenty-foot tree adorned with our favorite ornaments. Lots of our friends, like George Jones, Chet Atkins, and our band members with their families, along with our blended families would gather for fun and fellowship. I'd start playing the piano, and the toasting with eggnog would begin. Soon we'd all be singing Christmas favorites, new songs, old songs, whatever anyone wanted to sing. Those were the good ole days!

One year, we had been on the road so much with our shows that our assistant, Maureen Raffety, and the family had to pull the decorations together at the last minute. Helpers were scurrying up and down ladders and Shooter, our son, was helping Maureen and me hang ornaments. All of a sudden, Waylon walked through the room to check on our progress. We were proud of our elegant tree standing there in all its glory and waited for our review. Waylon looked up, tilted his head a bit to one side, and pronounced, "The tree's crooked." We all looked at him, then at each other, and we broke up laughing—it was just too funny. That was Waylon's way. It was his only contribution to our last-minute rush, but guess

what? He was right—the tree was crooked! Waylon Jennings sure lit up my world. Happy holidays and happy memories.

Light-Up-My-World Eggnog

This is wonderful eggnog to include in all of your Christmas holiday festivities. Serves 6 to 8

> 1 dozen large eggs
> 1 pint whipping cream
> 1 pint bourbon
> $\frac{1}{4}$ cup dark rum, such as Myers's
> 1 quart vanilla ice cream, softened
> 4 cups sugar

1. Separate the egg whites from the yolks, placing the whites in one large bowl and the yolks in another. Using electric beaters, whip the egg whites until soft peaks form. Set aside.

2. Place the cream in a large bowl. Using electric beaters, whip the cream until light and fluffy. Set aside.

3. Using electric beaters, beat the egg yolks until pale yellow in color. Add the bourbon and rum and continue beating the mixture until it is well blended. Beat in the ice cream and the sugar and continue beating until the sugar has dissolved and the mixture is no longer gritty. Transfer the mixture to a large punch bowl.

4. Using a large whisk or rubber spatula, whisk or fold in the whipped egg whites until they are incorporated. Then whisk or fold in the whipped cream until blended. To serve, ladle the eggnog into punch cups or small mugs.

Note: If children are going to be enjoying the eggnog, omit the bourbon and rum.

Waylon Jennings, Shooter, and Jessi

Donnie Fritts and Kris Kristofferson

A NATIVE OF FLORENCE, ALABAMA, Donnie Fritts grew up playing the drums with local bands. By the late 1950s, he was writing and performing with such outstanding talents as Arthur Alexander, Dan Penn, and Spooner Oldham. They all joined forces to forge the unique fusion of country, soul, country-pop, and R&B, which became recognized worldwide as the "Muscle Shoals" sound. Donnie's early songs were recorded by a diverse group of performers such as Percy Sledge, Dusty Springfield, The Box Tops, and Tommy Roe. In 1970, Donnie began touring as Kris Kristofferson's keyboardist. They appeared together in films including *Pat Garrett and Billy the Kid* and *A Star Is Born.*

Kris Kristofferson, songwriter, singer, and actor, has done it all. His songs have been major hits in virtually every genre of music, becoming international standards. He has appeared in a number of successful movies including *A Star Is Born,* with Barbra Streisand. His own recordings have sold millions. A member of the Country Music Hall of Fame, Kris continues a very full schedule of writing, performing, and acting.

Kris Kristofferson and Donnie Fritts

CHRISTMAS 1972, I was in Durango, Mexico, filming *Pat Garrett and Billy the Kid* with Kris Kristofferson. I lived with Kris; his fiancée, Rita Coolidge; and their housekeeper and cook, Maria, while we were shooting over the holidays. In the days leading up to Christmas, there was very little holiday spirit on the set—it just didn't feel like Christmas. I was hoping that would change when my wife, Donna, arrived a few days before Christmas to spend the holidays with me. Almost instantly, Donna and Maria hit it off and had a great time trading recipes. Maria taught Donna how to make tamales and Donna taught Maria how to make Southern banana pudding.

On Christmas Day, Sam Peckinpah, who was directing *Pat Garrett and Billy the Kid,* decided to have a party at his house for the cast and crew and their families. What a thrill to take a break from the movie work and sit back relaxing with Bob Dylan and James Coburn and their families and with the great character actors Gene Evans, Jack Elam, Matt Clark, and Harry Dean Stanton. I remember at one point, we decided we needed some more traditional Christmas décor at our party and before long, Kris and I were jumping into the back end of a pickup truck with some of the guys to find a Christmas tree.

Sam did make sure there were piñatas and donkey rides for the children, but part of that celebration was the wonderful Mexican food. We had turkey all right, but it was wrapped in banana leaves and roasted in a pit lined with hot coals. We also roasted a goat and a pig!

The party lasted all day and well into the night, with the dancing and singing led by a mariachi band. It was nothing like Christmas in Florence, Alabama, but it was certainly my most memorable one.

Good Friends Cheese Spread

Here's a real holiday party favorite! Pop open a pack of crackers and start spreading on some yummy Christmas cheer for the holidays. This is the perfect introduction for bringing together friends, old and new alike. Makes 3 quarts

> 2 pounds Velveeta cheese, cut into small chunks
> 8 ounces sharp Cheddar cheese, grated
> 8 ounces Swiss cheese, grated
> One (8-ounce) package cream cheese
> Three (7-ounce) jars diced pimientos, drained
> 3 cups Miracle Whip salad dressing, reduced-fat if desired

1. Combine the Velveeta, Cheddar, Swiss, and cream cheeses in a large bowl and let come to room temperature.

2. Add the pimientos and Miracle Whip. Using electric beaters, blend the mixture until it is completely smooth and creamy.

3. Spoon the cheese spread into small lidded glass or plastic containers. Seal well and refrigerate for up to 3 weeks.

Brenda Lee

BRENDA LEE made her first public appearance in 1950 at the age of five, winning an annual talent contest. This led to a yearlong regular appearance on *Starmakers Revue*, a popular Atlanta radio show. In 1956, after appearing on a number of local television shows, she made numerous appearances on the network show *Ozark Jubilee*. That year she also signed with Decca Records. Her early releases met with only moderate success, but the release of the song "Dynamite," coupled with her onstage enthusiasm, earned her the nickname Little Miss Dynamite. In 1959, Brenda broke onto the international scene with the song "Sweet Nothin's." She went on to become one of America's youngest and greatest superstars.

CHRISTMAS WAS ALWAYS a special day for me. We certainly didn't have much money, so the things we looked forward to were special treats like fruit and the toys my dad would make for us. A great whittler, he would make wooden cars and trains for my brother and little dolls for my sister and me. We would dress those dolls with pictures of clothes cut out from the Sears catalog.

I can remember wanting a bicycle so badly one year. My dad knew that and somehow managed to find an old, well-worn bike to fix up for me. He worked so hard to make that old bike look new. He painted it fire engine red; I didn't care that it was a boy's bike—it was the most beautiful thing I'd ever seen. That same year, I got a pair of little red cowboy boots to match. Now *that* was a Christmas to remember.

My family Christmases today always revolve around music and singing. My husband, Ronnie, and our two daughters started a tradition of Christmas caroling on December 24 and we never miss it. Another one of my favorite holiday traditions is decorating a special tree in our home I call the "fan Christmas tree." All the ornaments on the tree are from fans who have been touched in some way by my songs. I love to sing and share music, especially this time of year.

Rockin' Around the Tree with Salmon Balls

We love to sit around the tree, singing Christmas carols with our family and snacking on these tasty appetizers. Kick off your Christmas dinner with this new tradition. You'll be a-rockin' too.
Makes 24 salmon balls

3 pounds cooked salmon fillet, skin removed

1 cup cooked chickpeas

2 large eggs

1 cup finely chopped fresh spinach leaves

$1/3$ cup dried bread crumbs

$1/4$ cup minced fresh onion

1 tablespoon teriyaki sauce

Salt and cracked black pepper, to taste

2 tablespoons olive oil

1. Place the salmon and chickpeas in a large bowl. Using a potato masher, crush the fish and chickpeas until mashed. Add the eggs, spinach, bread crumbs, onion, and teriyaki sauce and stir until well blended. Season with salt and pepper to taste.

2. Using your hands, pinch off a bite-size portion of the salmon mixture and roll it into a ball. Continue pinching and rolling in this same manner until you have 24 balls. Place the balls in one or two con-tainers, cover, and refrigerate for at least 1 hour or until firm.

3. Working in two batches, place 1 tablespoon of oil in a large nonstick skillet over medium heat. When hot, add 12 of the salmon balls. Cook the balls, turning occasionally, for 10 minutes or until they are lightly browned and cooked through. Repeat the process with the remaining oil and salmon balls. Serve the balls warm.

Irlene Mandrell

ITH HER SISTERS Barbara and Louise, Irlene Mandrell appeared on the *Barbara Mandrell and The Mandrell Sisters* television series. She surprised everyone with her musical abilities and her penchant for comedy. When the Mandrell series ended, Irlene went on to become a regular on *Hee Haw;* she has also made many television appearances on shows such as *The Tonight Show, The Today Show,* and *Oprah.* She is involved in numerous charities and has been a national spokesperson for a number of companies. Irlene is married and has three children.

The Mandrell sisters, Irlene, Barbara, and Louise, with their father, Irby

CHRISTMAS is my favorite holiday. Not only is it a time to celebrate the birth of my Savior but it's also a time to celebrate my sister Barbara's birthday. Shortly before she was born, my father was told that neither the baby nor my mother, Mary, would survive childbirth. God granted our family two miracles that Christmas Day as both made it through the ordeal.

Many years later, I would experience my own Christmas miracle—the birth of my son, Deric, also on Christmas Day! Our family is now complete with two more miracles—my daughters, Vanessa and Christina, here to help us celebrate the greatest time of the year.

Drummer Girl Ham Croquettes and Cheese Sauce

Ham's doing double duty during the holidays. It's the center of the feast at the Christmas table, and the next day, it will be the star of the leftovers.
Serves 4

Croquettes

3 tablespoons margarine

$1/4$ cup unbleached, all-purpose flour

$3/4$ cup milk

2 cups diced cooked ham

1 teaspoon grated onion

Vegetable oil for deep-frying (about 4 cups)

1 cup crushed cornflakes or dried bread crumbs

1 large egg

Cheese Sauce

1 ($10^{1}/_{2}$-ounce) can cream of mushroom soup

5 (sandwich-size) slices American cheese

1. **To make the croquettes:** Melt the margarine in a medium saucepan over medium-high heat. Whisk in the flour and milk and cook, over medium-low heat, until the mixture is thick and bubbly, about 15 minutes.

2. Remove the saucepan from the heat and stir in the ham and onion. Transfer the mixture to a lidded container, seal, and refrigerate until firm, about 3 hours.

3. Place enough oil in a shallow medium saucepan to fill it halfway. Heat the oil over medium heat until it reaches 350°F. Test the oil by dropping in a small piece of fresh bread. If the bread rises and immediately turns golden, then the oil is hot enough.

4. Remove the ham mixture from the refrigerator. Using a large spoon, scoop up enough of the ham mixture to form a 2-inch oval croquette. Continue making croquettes in this same manner until you have used up all the ham mixture. You should have approximately 12 croquettes.

5. Place the cornflakes in a small bowl. Place the egg in another small bowl and whisk until smooth.

6. Dip each croquette in the egg mixture and then roll in the cornflakes. Working in batches (to prevent the oil from cooling down), drop 4 croquettes at a time in the oil and fry for 2 minutes, or until golden on both sides. Drain on a metal rack lined with a double layer of paper towels.

7. **To make the cheese sauce:** Combine the cream of mushroom soup with the cheese in a small saucepan. Place over medium-low heat and stir until the cheese has melted and blended into the soup. To serve, place 3 croquettes on each serving plate and top with the warm cheese sauce.

Dean Miller

*D*EAN MILLER, the son of the late singer/composer Roger Miller, launched his performing career as a solo act in the Santa Fe, New Mexico, club circuit. During his college days, he joined an acoustic group called the Sarcastic Hillbillies, while also pursuing a career in acting. After college, he moved to Nashville where he joined the songwriting staff of Sony Tree. In the late 1990s, he signed his first recording contract with Liberty Records. Dean continues to perform and to work in the music publishing business.

MY FATHER WROTE A SONG for and about me when I was young. The song was "Old Toy Trains." It became a Christmas classic and is still played every year at Christmastime. I recently went into the studio and recorded it as a duet with my father's tracks. In addition, I have recorded it again especially for the CD in this book.

A very special moment in my memory is on Christmas morning when I was fifteen years old; my clock radio went off and woke me up to "Old Toy Trains." It just doesn't get any better than that on Christmas Day.

Chip-off-the-Old-Block Miller Family Nachos

My father and I used to make a late-night snack of nachos in the toaster oven. We would take Doritos and put a spoonful of refried beans, a slice of cheese, and a jalapeño pepper on top. We would bake them in the oven for a few minutes until browned. Not much of a recipe, but it sure brings back memories! Serves 12

1 (16-ounce) bag corn chips, such as Doritos
1 (8-ounce) can refried beans
$\frac{1}{2}$ pound sliced Monterey Jack cheese
1 (6-ounce) jar pickled sliced jalapeño peppers, drained

1. Preheat the oven to 300°F.

2. Scatter the corn chips on a baking sheet. Spoon a portion of the refried beans onto each corn chip. Drape the cheese slices over the chips, and scatter the jalapeño peppers over the cheese. Bake the chips for 5 minutes, or until the cheese has melted and the nachos are hot.

Dean Miller with his father, Roger Miller

Tony Brown

ONY BROWN is a name associated with quality. After working as a road musician for such acts as the Stamps Quartet, the Blackwoods, the Oak Ridge Boys, and Elvis Presley, Tony accepted an A&R job in 1979 with RCA Records. There he signed such acts as Alabama and Vince Gill, and he established himself as a record producer. In 1984, he moved to MCA Records, where he signed such alternative country artists as Steve Earl, Lyle Lovett, and Nanci Griffith. He recorded successful albums with superstars like George Strait, Reba McEntire, Trisha Yearwood, and Wynonna Judd.

Today, Tony is a partner with Tim Dubois at Universal South Records. Among all of his successes, Tony counts as his greatest accomplishment his marriage with Anastasia. Anastasia is one of the most successful female business leaders in the Nashville music industry. She is recognized for her grasp of all aspects of popular culture, including music, television, and fashion.

Tony Brown with his wife, Anastasia, and son, Wilson

I GREW UP in Winston-Salem, North Carolina, with my parents, sister, and two brothers. My family was very poor, but I never knew it. When my father was diagnosed with lung cancer and lost his job, Mom went to work in a dress shop.

At Christmastime, our next-door neighbors got new bikes with every gadget that you could get on a bike. Our bikes came from the Goodwill store, but we thought they were just as good. In fact, all our presents came from Goodwill, but I never thought anything about it—presents are presents.

Some things are different now at Christmastime. My wife, Anastasia, and I enjoy a huge fifteen-foot silver spruce Christmas tree in the living room. It is very glamorous with ribbons wrapped around it and beautiful ornaments decorating the limbs. We started hanging Christmas stockings when we had kids of our own.

Some things, however, are much the same as when I grew up in Winston-Salem. We love opening presents on Christmas morning with our children, and we still leave a plate of cookies and a glass of milk for Santa to enjoy (which, of course, he does).

When I think of what's happening in the world today, I recall these words that seem very appropriate for this time of year. Let there be peace on earth. Merry Christmas.

Piano Man Old-Fashioned Vegetable Soup

I'm playing a happy tune when the aroma of this old-fashioned favorite drifts in my way. There's nothing better than sipping on a bowl of hot vegetable soup after a chilly evening of Christmas caroling. Serves 10

  3 tablespoons vegetable oil
  2 pounds stewing meat, cut into bite-size cubes
  1 small onion, diced
  1 green bell pepper, diced
  1 garlic clove, crushed
  5 medium potatoes, peeled and diced
  3 (15-ounce) cans mixed vegetables with liquid
  1 (15-ounce) can okra with liquid
  Salt and cracked black pepper, to taste
  2 cups beef broth
  3 tablespoons sugar

1. Heat the oil in a soup pot over medium heat. Add the meat, onion, bell pepper, and garlic and cook until the meat has browned, 5 to 7 minutes.

2. Add the potatoes, mixed vegetables and their liquid, and okra and its liquid. Season the soup with salt and pepper to taste. Bring the mixture to a simmer, reduce the heat to low, and cook for 20 minutes. Stir in the broth and sugar and simmer the soup for 2$1/2$ hours. Season with additional salt and black pepper to taste.

Ray Price

RAY PRICE is one of the most resilient performers in country music. His recording career started in late 1949 when he made his first record for the Nashville-based Bullet label. He started performing on Dallas radio programs, including the popular *Big D Jamboree* on station KRLD. Troy Martin, a Peer-Southern Publishing executive, heard Ray and secured him a contract with Columbia Records. He joined the *Grand Ole Opry* in 1952, roomed with Hank Williams Sr. for a time, and shared Hank's Drifting Cowboys as his band. Ray's early records reveal Hank's influences. Then, in 1956, Ray had a number one record with "Crazy Arms." A string of hits followed, and in the mid-1960s he diversified his style by recording pop-flavored ballads such as "Make the World Go Away," "For the Good Times," and Willie Nelson's "Night Life." A whole new career began as he climbed farther up the country and pop ladder with each release.

Ray Price with his wife, Janie

THE BEST CHRISTMAS I can remember is when I lived on the farm. There were eleven of us in one house including my dad, my brother, my aunts and uncles, and my grandparents. We went out in the woods and cut down a tree and brought it home. We decorated the tree with popcorn balls and strings of popcorn. My grandmother had a star she saved for the top, and she religiously saved angel hair. That was in the 1930s and times were tough for farmers like my granddad. So we didn't get much in the way of presents. But we did each make a gift for the person whose name we drew. Finding out who you were getting a gift for was fun. This kind of Christmas was the real thing. Our Christmas stockings were hung on the fireplace mantel and when we woke up, each one got a lot of fruit and one toy. For some it was homemade, for others it was store bought. I remember my gift was a pocket knife—and you know every farm boy needs a pocket knife! I'm eighty years old and I still treasure that memory today.

Christmas dinner was always a big deal. We always ate what we grew and canned, and our Christmas ham came from pigs we raised. The ladies would prepare the best meal in the world. Those early Christmas memories sure are strong.

For the Good Times Classic Onion Soup

Janie and I really enjoy a hot bowl of soup. This is a simple recipe, but it is full of flavor. This onion soup is the perfect beginning to our holiday meal, or anytime there's a chill in the air. Serves 6

> 4 tablespoons ($\frac{1}{2}$ stick) unsalted butter,
>   plus 2 tablespoons, softened, for buttering
>   the bread
> 4 cups thinly sliced white onions
> 1 garlic clove, minced
> $5\frac{1}{2}$ cups beef broth
> $\frac{1}{2}$ cup dry white wine or sherry
> Salt and cracked black pepper, to taste
> 6 (1-inch-thick) slices French bread
> 6 ($\frac{1}{4}$-inch-thick) slices Gruyère or provolone cheese,
>   large enough to cover the French bread

1. Preheat the oven to 325°F.

2. Place the 4 tablespoons of butter in a large saucepan over medium heat. When melted, add the onions and garlic and sauté until golden, about 10 minutes.

3. Stir in the broth and wine and bring the mixture to a boil. Reduce the heat to low and simmer for 5 minutes. Season the soup with salt and black pepper to taste.

4. Arrange 6 ovenproof soup bowls on a baking sheet. Ladle an even portion of the soup into each bowl. Butter each slice of French bread and place one slice in the center of each soup bowl. Lay a piece of cheese over each slice of bread. Bake the soup for 5 minutes, or until the cheese begins to melt and brown around the edges.

Terre Thomas

ERRE THOMAS grew up hearing about St. Jude from her father, television icon Danny Thomas. She has been a member of the ALSAC/St. Jude Board of Directors and Governors since 1980, participating in decisions that led to the hospital's recent expansion. She has been a spokesperson for the hospital, a role that came naturally to her as a result of her familiarity with the organization. She writes country music, sings frequently on behalf of St. Jude, and appears across the United States for the Country Cares for St. Jude Kids radiothons.

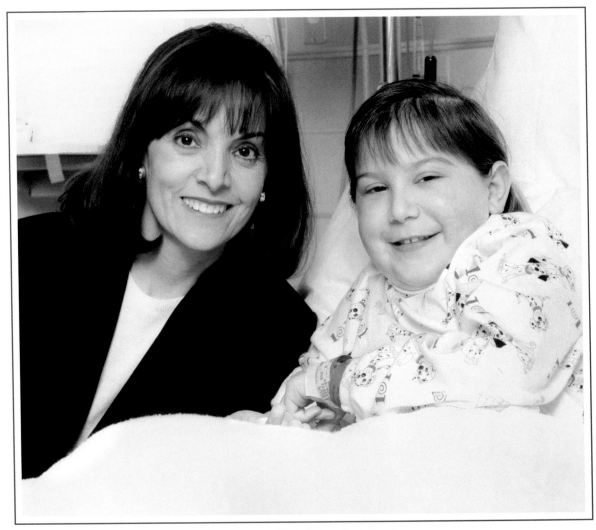

Terre Thomas with St. Jude patient Claudia

MY FAVORITE Christmas story is kind of a two-act play. Around Christmas 1947, I asked Santa Claus for twin baby brothers—one for me and one for my sister, Marlo. Somehow, I didn't figure Mom into the equation, except I did ask Santa for lots of diapers for her to use. I remember asking Mom if it was okay to ask Santa for this gift, and without hesitation, she simply said, "Yes." I can still remember the look on her face, and I remember thinking her answer came very quickly for such a large, important gift. She didn't even flinch or question the number of babies I requested.

Well, Christmas came and Christmas went and no babies! Mom did start putting on a little weight throughout the year, though! Well, wouldn't you know that the next Christmas, along came the very thing I had asked for the year before—a baby brother, named Tony. Okay, so it wasn't twins, but I didn't care! There was this adorable creature for my sister and me to pamper and play with while Mom was doing the diapers, of course (just like I'd planned). So, wishes can come true—big time! You just have to know who to ask.

Make Room for Sweet Potato, Peanut Butter, Curry Soup

This is my favorite recipe and it's perfect for those days when autumn and winter bring the lower temperatures to your house. Put on a big pot; you'll love it too. Serves 8

4 medium orange sweet potatoes or yams
Olive oil for rubbing
Salt and cracked black pepper, to taste
2 tablespoons unsalted butter
1 large onion, chopped
5 garlic cloves, minced
4 (14-ounce) cans low-sodium chicken broth
1 (6-ounce) jar creamy peanut butter
1 tablespoon allspice
1 tablespoon curry powder, or more to taste

1. Preheat the oven to 400°F.

2. Place the sweet potatoes on a baking sheet and rub each potato with enough olive oil to coat. Season the potatoes with salt and pepper to taste and bake for 45 minutes, or until a sharp knife easily pierces through the center of one potato. When cool enough to handle, remove the skin from each potato and set aside the flesh.

3. Place the butter in a soup pot over medium heat. When melted, add the onion and garlic and sauté until the onion is soft, about 10 minutes. Add the chicken broth, peanut butter, allspice, curry powder, and sweet potato flesh. Bring the mixture to a boil, reduce the heat to low, and simmer, covered, for 1 hour.

4. Using an immersion blender, purée the soup until smooth. (Alternatively, purée the soup in a blender until smooth and transfer back to the soup pot.) Season the soup with salt, pepper, and additional curry powder to taste. Serve hot.

Edie Hand

EDIE HAND is an author, a professional cook, a businesswoman, an inspirational speaker, and a television and radio personality. Edie was featured in the daytime soap opera *As the World Turns;* is currently the host of the show *Southern Style with Edie and Friends;* and regularly appears on local, regional, and national television. A three-time cancer survivor, she shares her story of triumph through her inspirational and motivational speaking engagements.

Her books include *All Cooked Up,* a book of recipes and memories of growing up around the entertainment business with her legendary cousin, Elvis Presley.

Edie lives near Birmingham, Alabama. Her actor son, Linc Hand, lives in Los Angeles, California.

THE WEEK BEFORE CHRISTMAS in 1969, as my grandmother and I set out to drive from Red Bay, Alabama, to Memphis, Tennessee, snow began falling. By the time we reached Graceland, winter's new white blanket had settled onto everything and was reflecting what must have been thousands of lights nestled among every tree and shrub on the property. The only thing more spectacular to this wide-eyed teenager was what waited inside: the largest and most beautiful Christmas tree I had ever seen.

As we entered Graceland, we stood in the magnificent foyer looking to our left, into the dining

Edie Hand with her son, Linc

room. I was awestruck by the royal blue draperies trimmed in gold, walls adorned with beautiful mirrors, and a sparkling Austrian crystal chandelier. Aunt Dodger was sitting at the lace-covered dining room table. I asked Grandma Alice and Aunt Dodger, "How come there are so many presents around this humongous tree?" They both smiled and said at the same time, "Because Elvis loves to give to others!" Aunt Dodger said, "Child, if you'll always be willing to help those in need, you'll be blessed a hundredfold by the Lord. Elvis's gifts will light up with hope as many faces as there are lights around Graceland this Christmas." Then she said, "Enough talking, let's go eat some of Mary's famous tapioca pudding." Mary Jenkins was one of the best cooks at Graceland.

Then I heard Elvis's voice as he came down the stairs. When he entered the room he hugged everyone, and I impatiently waited my turn. Finally, I got my warm hug from Elvis. He asked if we were going to eat and talk all afternoon or did we want to buy more presents for him to give away. Within the hour, Grandma Alice and I were out the door with Aunt Nash, heading to the local department store to buy more surprises for others.

I wanted to buy Elvis a gift, so Aunt Nash helped me pick out a handsome pair of black silk pajamas that she was sure Elvis would love.

When we returned to Graceland with shopping bags spilling over with gifts, we saw Elvis and Uncle Vernon in the seven-car carport area loading a wheelchair into one of Elvis's cars. Elvis had heard of a family in need of a new wheelchair, and he had had one sent over to Graceland so he could personally deliver it!

My grandmother Alice said, "Elvis, we'll be leaving shortly to get Edie back home." He said, "Don't leave till Daddy and I get back." My heart was so happy. I couldn't believe he was really a part of my family!

Elvis and Uncle Vernon returned shortly as promised. They met us in Dodger's room where we were listening to Grandma Alice's never-ending ghost stories.

I'll always remember each face at that moment in her room. Elvis began handing out gifts, and I heard myself saying, "But it's not Christmas yet." He looked right at me and leaned forward as if he were sharing a treasured secret and said, "Christmas can be anytime." I was thrilled watching all the ladies receive their gifts of jewelry and was surprised when Elvis handed me a perfectly wrapped box like theirs. In it was a necklace and earring set, made of unique blue and purple crystals that he had purchased in Hawaii. I still get them out every Christmas and enjoy sharing the memory of this genuine gift to me from Elvis, so the legacy will live on with my son, Linc.

Living the Legacy Layered Vegetable Salad

My husband and son both love salads, and this is one of their favorites. It will be a welcome addition to your Christmas feast or anytime throughout the holidays when you need to take a break from too many rich dishes. It looks as good as it tastes, too. Serves 12

4 cups mixed salad greens
2 medium zucchini, trimmed and thinly sliced
2 celery stalks, thinly sliced
2 cups chopped raw cauliflower
1 red bell pepper, cored, seeded, and chopped
1 (10-ounce) package frozen petit peas, thawed
1/4 cup chopped fresh parsley
1 cup mayonnaise
1 cup sour cream
3 tablespoons Dijon mustard
1 tablespoon minced fresh rosemary
1 tablespoon minced fresh oregano
2 teaspoons garlic salt
Salt and cracked black pepper, to taste
2 cups shredded Cheddar cheese
1/2 pound bacon, cooked and crumbled
1/2 cup thinly sliced scallions

1. Arrange the salad greens in the bottom of a very large salad bowl or a 6-quart serving dish. Working in layers, scatter the zucchini over the greens, followed by the celery, cauliflower, bell pepper, peas, and parsley.

2. Blend together the mayonnaise, sour cream, mustard, rosemary, oregano, and garlic salt in a small bowl. Season with pepper and additional salt to taste. Pour the dressing evenly over the salad. Sprinkle the cheese over the salad, followed by the bacon and scallions. Cover the salad and chill for several hours in the refrigerator before serving.

Bill Mack

*W*HEN HE WAS SEVENTEEN, Bill Mack got his first broadcasting job at his hometown radio station, KEVA, in Shamrock, Texas. His duties included cleaning the bathroom and vacuuming the floors, before going on the air for an hour. For this, he received $12.50 per week. His big break came in 1969 when he was offered the midnight to six A.M. show on the powerhouse WBAP in Fort Worth, Texas. Calling himself "The Midnight Cowboy," for thirty-two years Bill endeared himself to truckers, entertainers, and fans across the country. He joined XM Satellite Radio in September 2001, where he renamed himself "The XM Satellite Cowboy." Bill has written over three hundred songs, but is especially proud of his award-winning composition "Blue," which made LeAnn Rimes a star and won a Grammy for Country Song of the Year. Bill has achieved his place among the giants, and he deserves it.

CHRISTMAS IN THE 1930s was different from what it is today. The same carols are sung and there haven't been many changes in Christmas trees or decorations. The main difference that I see is in the toys. A youngster during the 1930s didn't have the opportunity to enjoy computerized games. Even if the computer had been invented, most families wouldn't have been able to afford one. After all, America was still affected by the Great Depression. If you had an electric train set, there was no doubt that your dad had a good paying job. In my house, if you didn't wind it, it didn't work!

My big wish for years was for a bicycle. How-

Bill Mack with his family

ever, the price for a bike was way beyond the means of my dad, who drove a truck, hauling cottonseed.

When I was seven years old, I was with my dad at Benson Hardware in my hometown of Shamrock. Standing on a special shelf in the middle of the big room was the most beautiful yellow bike I had ever seen! I felt my dad's hand on my shoulder. "Someday," he said.

As Christmas drew nearer, my parents called my brother and me into the living room. Handing us hot chocolate, Mom asked, "What do you want from Santa this year?" I can't remember what wishes I revealed; however, I didn't ask for a bicycle. I knew my wish would simply hurt my dad. My little brother, who was only three years old, asked for a little red tricycle among other things.

Christmas Eve, I went with my dad to shop for Mom's gift, a new kitchen stove. As we entered Benson Hardware, I noticed the yellow bike was no longer on display. As we left the building, he placed his hand on my shoulder. This time, he didn't say anything.

It was a cold Christmas morning as my brother and I awoke to the smell of Mom fixing our special breakfast on her new stove. We anxiously ran to the Christmas tree, noticing that it was loaded with various little wind-up toys. My little brother's red tricycle was standing proudly in the center of the room. As he screamed with joy, I felt genuinely happy for him.

After opening the various gifts, we walked into the dining room for our Christmas breakfast. Pop offered the blessing. Then he looked at me and asked, "Would you go get me a knife from the kitchen? I'll need it to cut the ham."

I walked into the kitchen, pulled a big knife from the drawer, and as I turned to go back into the dining room I saw a yellow glow. The bike leaned against the door to the hallway. A big note was taped to the seat: "Your SOMEDAY has come! SANTA."

Talkin' Country Potato Salad

Christmas was always a big event at our house. We always looked forward to the toys, but the delicious food that was prepared still stands out in my mind, especially Mom's potato salad.
Serves 6

1½ pounds waxy potatoes, peeled and cut into
   small chunks
3 large eggs
2 celery stalks, thinly sliced
1 medium red onion, chopped
1 red bell pepper, cored, seeded, and chopped
¼ cup sweet pickle relish
3 tablespoons mayonnaise, reduced-fat if desired
1½ teaspoons prepared mustard
1 (2-ounce) jar pimientos, drained
Salt and cracked black pepper, to taste

1. Bring a medium saucepan of water to a boil. Add the potatoes and cook over medium-low heat until tender when pierced with a sharp knife, about 15 minutes. Drain and let cool.

2. While the potatoes are cooking, bring a small saucepan of water to a boil. Add the eggs and gently boil for 12 minutes. Drain, cool, and then peel.

3. Combine the cooled potatoes with the celery, onion, and bell pepper. Chop two of the hard-cooked eggs and add to the potato mixture.

4. Stir together the pickle relish, mayonnaise, mustard, and pimientos in a small bowl. Add to the potato salad and gently toss to mix. Season with salt and pepper to taste. Cut the remaining egg into slices and arrange over the potato salad. Cover and chill in the refrigerator before serving.

Ronnie McDowell

RONNIE MCDOWELL is one of those artists who can say about his audience, "Once a fan, always a fan." His genuine warmth and sincerity leave a lingering effect on those whose paths he crosses. Ronnie exploded on the music scene in 1977 when he recorded his heartfelt tribute song to Elvis Presley, "The King Is Gone." Almost overnight, he became a superstar in both pop and country circles across the United States and around the world. His string of hits continued with "I Love You, I Love You, I Love You," "Watchin' Girls Go By," "Older Women," and many other top-ten recordings. Ronnie lives in Nashville, Tennessee, and continues to charm his audiences wherever he performs.

GROWING UP, I often envied the lavish gifts that other kids received at Christmas. With ten children in the family, there was not a lot of money for nonessentials. We were usually happy to receive a stocking full of oranges, some candy, maybe a pair of pants. But there was one year that I was the kid to envy. Rexall Consumers Drugs in my hometown of Portland, Tennessee, was having a contest: Those who turned in receipts of the most money spent from September to Christmas Eve would receive a brand-new battery-powered airplane. The toy sat in the display window, large and shiny. I was eight years old, and I had a mission.

I began by collecting my mother's receipts, then solicited other family members, and eventually expanded my efforts to include any willing donor. I collected dozens of receipts weekly and eagerly presented them to the store manager. There was a poster that charted the progress and I watched my name climb up the list, from seventh to fifth to third. Finally, on Christmas Eve 1958, I was in second place. I spent the entire day standing outside the door, smiling and soliciting.

That afternoon, a new name went to the top of the list and it was mine! I had 638 points. When they handed me the airplane I felt like the luckiest kid in the world. I walked home, carrying my prize and grinning.

Now I enjoy making Christmas memories for other children. Every Christmas my son, Tyler, and I take about thirty kids on my tour bus to Wal-Mart for an afternoon of buying presents and having fun. Each kid gets to spend $100 for Christmas (you would be surprised to see what they buy: presents for Grandma, Grandpa, brother, sister, etc.). Then we head to McDonald's for a fun meal. It's so fulfilling to see these kids enjoy their day and return to share their adventure with their families.

Sing-for-the-King Corn Salad

What's a Christmas dinner without this golden nugget? This festive salad is a special way to bring some summer sunshine into your holiday dining room. Serves 10 to 12

    2 (12-ounce) cans shoepeg corn, drained
    2 tomatoes, chopped
    1 green bell pepper, cored, seeded, and chopped
    1 small red onion, chopped
    1 cucumber, peeled and chopped
    $\frac{1}{2}$ cup sour cream
    $\frac{1}{4}$ cup mayonnaise
    2 tablespoons white vinegar
    $\frac{1}{2}$ teaspoon celery seed
    $\frac{1}{2}$ teaspoon dry mustard
    Salt and cracked black pepper, to taste

1. Combine the corn, tomatoes, bell pepper, onion, and cucumber in a salad bowl. Toss to mix.

2. Blend together the sour cream, mayonnaise, vinegar, celery seed, and dry mustard in a small bowl. Pour over the salad and gently toss to blend. Season with salt and black pepper to taste.

Michael Peterson

BEFORE HIS SUCCESS as a country singer, Michael Peterson spent twelve years as a motivational speaker, inspiring hundreds of thousands of teenagers in public schools across North America. He is a proven people mover with a purpose bigger than himself. In 1997, he burst onto the country music scene with his album *Michael Peterson* on Reprise Records. The album boasted three number-one CMT music videos and five consecutive top-twenty radio hits, including the number one smash "From Here to Eternity." He was named top new artist of 1997 by both *Billboard* and *Radio and Records.* Michael maintains a very active schedule as a performer and speaker. Along with his many charities, Michael is also heavily involved each year with Trees for Troops.

I WAS STUCK. Stuck in a cab in downtown Toronto in the dead of winter with a driver who insisted on playing "A Partridge in a Pear Tree" over and over. But after the third listen I started to make up my own words:

> *Eight flights with layovers*
> *Seven fries with Big Macs*
> *Six dull hotel rooms*
> *FIVE SOLD-OUT SHOWS*
> *Four more days to go*
> *Three lost bags*
> *Too tired to speak*
> *and a cabbie who's driving too slow.*

Staring out the back window at one more red light on my way from the airport to my next hotel, I saw something I had never seen before. It was a man wrapped up in a cardboard blanket, lying against the cold brick of the Eaton Center shopping mall. From the bottom of the cardboard I saw bare feet protruding. It was snowing. Just then the light changed, and we passed by.

The next morning I arrived at the television station early to prepare for my interview. While

waiting in the green room I met the janitor, who informed me that he knew how cold it was because he rode his bike to work. He told me that he had been feeling a bit sorry for himself . . . that is, until that morning when he saw a man sleeping

on the sidewalk in a cardboard box with no shoes down by the Eaton Center.

He told me he knew he had to help the man, so he parked his bike and went into the mall to buy the man some socks and shoes. Because of that he was behind on his job and had to excuse himself. He smiled at me and said, "Merry Christmas."

Just then I was called to my interview and as I was walking toward the set I heard the tail end of the interview that preceded me. It was a story about Mother Teresa who, when asked how she did so many great things with her life, answered by saying she did not believe any of us could do great things alone, but we could all do small things with great love.

That moment and her voice have stayed with me for fifteen years or so . . . calling me to a purpose bigger than myself.

Over the years, I have learned that the smallest good deed is better than the grandest intention, which is why I am doing all I can during Christmas to help the Christmas Spirit Foundation, the New Holland Company, and Federal Express to send live trees to soldiers in the desert as a reminder of home.

It's my way of saying, "I hope you know you are never forgotten."

Modern Man's Chicken Salad with Ranch Dressing

Holidays and Grandmother's house always meant lots of wonderful foods. She put plenty of love in all that she did, but the holiday foods were exceptional. My family and I celebrate the holidays just like Grandmother. We spread lots of love by doing little things in big ways and big things in little ways. Hope you enjoy one of our healthy holiday dishes. Serves 8

Chicken Salad

4 cups diced cooked chicken

1 (16-ounce) bottle teriyaki sauce

1 cup chopped celery

$1/2$ cup diced yellow bell pepper

$1/2$ cup thinly sliced scallions

2 tablespoons chopped pimiento

$1/2$ cup whole roasted cashews

4 medium tomatoes, sliced

Dressing

1 cup buttermilk

$1/2$ cup prepared salsa

3 tablespoons reduced-fat mayonnaise

2 tablespoons chopped fresh parsley

1 tablespoon fresh lemon juice

$1/2$ teaspoon sugar

$1/2$ teaspoon dry mustard

$1/4$ teaspoon salt

$1/4$ teaspoon cracked black pepper

1. To make the chicken salad: Place the chicken in a medium bowl and toss with the teriyaki sauce. Let marinate for 15 minutes; drain.

2. Add the celery, bell pepper, scallions, and pimiento to the marinated chicken and toss to mix.

3. To make the dressing: Place the buttermilk, salsa, mayonnaise, parsley, lemon juice, sugar, dry mustard, salt, and black pepper in a blender and blend until smooth.

4. To serve, add the cashews to the chicken salad and toss with as much buttermilk dressing as desired. (Save the remaining salad dressing in a lidded jar and store in the refrigerator for up to 2 weeks.) Arrange several tomato slices on each serving plate, overlapping the tomatoes slightly to form a circular "base." Spoon some of the chicken salad into the center portion of the tomato circle.

Jim Stafford

JIM STAFFORD'S comic genius has placed him at the forefront of America's greatest entertainers with songs like "Spiders and Snakes," "My Girl Bill," "Wildwood Weed," and "Cow Patti." Jim launched his television career in 1975 with the *Jim Stafford Show* on ABC. His numerous television appearances include twenty-six times on *The Tonight Show* and co-hosting *Those Amazing Animals* with Burgess Meredith. He also worked as performer, writer, and producer on the *Smothers Brothers Comedy Hour*. Jim owns a state-of-the-art theater in Branson, Missouri, where he performs nightly to sold-out crowds. His amazing ability to continue producing fresh material makes him one of the most durable entertainers around.

Jim Stafford with his family: Allie, Annie, Shea, and GG

I REMEMBER VERY WELL the Christmas season I was five years old. A few days before Christmas, I started playing with a box of matches and set our house on fire. With the exception of some smoke inhalation, I escaped unharmed; however, the entire house burned down. So there we were, a couple days before Christmas with no home, no belongings, no presents, nothing.

But in the end we had a very beautiful Christmas because our neighbors took us in and shared their Christmas with us, presents and all. And not just the next-door neighbors, but the whole neighborhood. What a wonderful lesson that was, of how those around you who know what you need are there to take care of you, and that your family extends beyond your next of kin.

That Christmas became our own version of *The Christmas Story*. I was so young at the time that I don't even remember if I apologized to Dad for burning down his house. Later he said, "Son, I only needed half of the money they gave me to rebuild that little house. I used the other half to start my own business. So don't you feel bad: You didn't get hurt; we found out what wonderful, loving neighbors we had; and your daddy became an independent businessman." Then Dad said, "The Lord sure does work in mysterious ways." I felt so relieved after all those years. When I became successful, one of the first things I did was buy my folks a house.

Cow Patti's Cherry Salad

Ask Glen Campbell how great this dish is. At our house, he fills up his bowl and eats it with a big ole soupspoon. That oughta be proof enough, but you try it yourself. Next time you'll be grabbing a bigger bowl. Just get there before Glen shows up. Serves 12

1 (15½-ounce) can dark pitted sweet cherries with juice
1 (7½-ounce) can crushed pineapple, drained
1 cup pecans, chopped
1 (8-ounce) package cream cheese
1 (6-ounce) box cherry gelatin
2 cups cold cola soft drink
12 lettuce leaves for serving

1. Saving the juice, drain the cherries. Set the juice aside and cut each cherry in half. Scatter the cherry halves, crushed pineapple, and pecans across the bottom of a 13 by 9-inch baking dish. Cut the cream cheese into bite-size chunks and evenly scatter them over the fruit and nut mixture.

2. Place the reserved cherry juice in a medium saucepan and bring to a boil. Stir in the cherry gelatin mix. Turn off the heat and stir the gelatin mixture until it begins to cool and thicken. Blend in the cola and pour over the fruit and nut mixture. Seal the dish with plastic wrap and chill in the refrigerator for several hours, or until completely gelled. To serve, cut the gelatin mixture into brownie-size squares and serve on lettuce leaves.

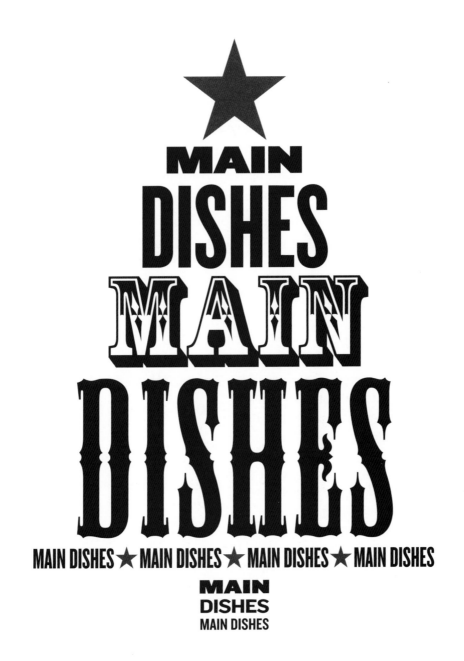

MAIN
DISHES
MAIN
DISHES

MAIN DISHES ★ MAIN DISHES ★ MAIN DISHES ★ MAIN DISHES

MAIN
DISHES
MAIN DISHES

Clint Black and Lisa Hartman Black

$\mathcal{I}$N 1989, a song called "A Better Man" introduced a talented and personable young man from Texas to the lovers of country music. Clint Black, with his Cheshire cat grin and songs about life, touched the hearts of the record-buying public, scoring five number-one singles on his debut album, which went triple platinum. That album and successive releases, which also became million-copy sellers, catapulted Clint up there with the big boys, garnering many honors and awards. At a hometown show in Houston, he met Houston-born actress Lisa Hartman. In 1991, he joined the cast of the *Grand Ole Opry.* In September of that year he and Lisa announced their engagement. In October of that same year, the two were wed. Lisa and Clint have one child, a daughter named Lily.

OUR FAVORITE Christmas memories now center around our beautiful daughter, Lily. She loves the Christmas lights. She's intrigued by the colors and wonders what causes the tree lights to flash on and off.

The family enjoys watching her wide-eyed excitement as she tears into gift after gift, barely getting one gift open before reaching for another one. Her excitement over receiving a scooter from Santa and wanting to take it outside immediately, even in the snow, took us back to our own childhoods and made us feel like kids again.

Lily's excitement at Christmas makes us all look forward to the next one where again we can share Christmas through a child's eyes.

Lovebirds' Roasted Rosemary Chicken

Christmastime cooking at our house includes this wonderful chicken dish. The rosemary adds a special touch, and the aroma while the bird is roasting makes it one of our favorite holiday dishes. Serves 4

1 (3- to 4-pound) roasting chicken

2 tablespoons olive oil

5 sprigs rosemary

Salt and cracked black pepper, to taste

1 lemon

2 parsnips, peeled and cut into chunks, optional

2 carrots, peeled and cut into chunks, optional

1 large red onion, peeled and cut into eighths

1 cup chicken broth

1. Preheat the oven to 450°F.

2. Rinse the chicken under cold water and pat dry with paper towels. Rub 1 tablespoon of the oil all over the bird and then place it in a roasting pan.

3. Tuck one rosemary sprig in the cavity of the bird and mince the remaining 4 sprigs. Sprinkle half of the minced rosemary over the bird, then season it with salt and pepper to taste. Cut the lemon in half and squeeze the juice of one lemon half over the bird and the juice of the other lemon half into the bird's cavity. Place the juiced lemon halves inside the bird.

4. Combine the parsnips and carrots, if using, in a medium bowl with the onion. Toss with the remain-ing 1 tablespoon of oil and remaining minced rosemary. Scatter the vegetables around the chicken and roast for 30 minutes, basting the chicken with any accumulated juices.

5. Pour the chicken broth over the vegetables and continue roasting the chicken, basting occasionally, until an instant-read thermometer inserted into the thickest part of the thigh reads approximately 165°F, 45 to 50 minutes more. Remove the bird from the oven and let rest for 10 minutes before carving and serving with the vegetables.

Clint Black and Lisa Hartman Black with their daughter, Lily

Cheryl Rogers-Barnett

CHERYL ROGERS-BARNETT was adopted by cowboy movie star Roy Rogers and his first wife, Arline, in 1940. Cheryl appeared in *Trail of Robin Hood,* one of her dad's movies, and one episode of his television series *The Roy Rogers Show.* As a teenager, Cheryl tried singing professionally for a short time. She was a charter member of Child Help USA, an organization that leads the national battle against child abuse, and she serves on the executive committee of the Golden Boot Awards and numerous other organizations. Cheryl has written a memoir, *Cowboy Princess.* In it she relates her life growing up with world-famous parents. She and her husband Larry appear at western festivals across the country.

I DON'T THINK Dad had many, if any, Christmas trees as a kid growing up in the hills of eastern Ohio; at least he never spoke of one. That's probably why our Christmas trees meant as much to him as the presents they sheltered.

The first Christmas that he and Mom (Dale Evans) were married, we had recently moved into a beautiful home in the Hollywood Hills that had once belonged to silent movie star Noah Beery. It had a wonderful high ceiling and a huge picture window in the living room. Dad found a beautiful tree, and he and Mom found the most beautiful white ornaments. We put tons of tinsel on it until the whole tree shimmered. Mom decided that since Dad found the tree for the living room, she would get small trees for Linda, Dusty, and me. They were very small blue trees with very small white ornaments and we thought they were the most beautiful trees we had ever seen—until the next year.

Dad decided to get an even bigger and better tree. He went somewhere in Hollywood and found the most incredible tree that I have ever seen, either before or since! Dad loved having the tree flocked so that it looked as though it had just been brought in out of the snow. This place had the most unusual flocking you can imagine; he may have even gotten it from a set decorator. It was flocked with duck down that had shiny crystal-like flakes mixed in the flocking; Mom and Dad put all white lights on it so that it looked like a fairy tree. I do remember, however, Dad saying that it cost a small fortune and that we should keep it up as long as we safely could because we probably would never have one that expensive again.

The next year Dad found another beautiful green tree and told us he found out how he could simulate our beautiful down-flocked tree of the past year. He said someone had told him that you put Ivory Flakes in a big bowl with a little bit of water, beat the mixture with a kitchen mixer until it gets light and fluffy, then spread it on the branches of the tree, and sprinkle more dry Ivory Flakes to get the glittery shine of the crystals. Mom didn't want us to use an electric mixer for fear that we would electrocute ourselves, so we used an old hand-crank kind. Linda Lou, who was six, and I helped Dad crank that thing, trying to make the stuff "light and fluffy," but all we managed to achieve was "heavy and soggy." We

Roy Rogers's Cowboy Chocolate Chili

Cowboys love hearty, tasty grub after a long day on the range. Chili is an easy but traditional dish, especially by the campfire; but with a house full of children at home adding the extra-special chocolate made it seem like you were having dessert first. **Serves 6**

> 3 pounds ground beef
> 1 pound pork loin, diced
> 2 (28-ounce) cans diced tomatoes
> 4 bay leaves
> 4 garlic cloves, minced
> 2 tablespoons chili powder
> 4 teaspoons ground cumin
> 1 teaspoon dried oregano
> Salt and cracked black pepper, to taste
> 2 teaspoons unbleached, all-purpose flour
> 2 ounces semisweet chocolate, grated

cranked some more and got the first batch looking a little better, but when we spread it on the branches it weighed so much that the branches drooped almost immediately. After a couple more batches, Dad realized that we would never have enough to cover the tree and he decided to take the stuff off the tree. Soon we had the most peculiar-looking tree ever. After that, he had the trees flocked where he bought them.

We always had beautiful trees, but I've never forgotten our beautiful down-covered tree, and my grandchildren love hearing the story about Great-Grandpa and the most beautiful Christmas tree ever.

1. Place a large nonstick skillet over medium-high heat. Add the beef and pork to the dry skillet and cook until browned, about 10 minutes. Drain off any excess fat.

2. Stir in the tomatoes, bay leaves, garlic, chili powder, cumin, and oregano; season with salt and pepper to taste. Sprinkle the flour over the mixture and stir to blend. Bring the chili to a boil, reduce the heat to low, and simmer, covered, for 1 hour.

3. Blend in the chocolate and stir until melted. Continue cooking the chili over low heat for 10 more minutes to meld the flavors. Remove the bay leaves and serve.

Jessy Dixon

JESSY DIXON has done it all. As a songwriter he has created a gigantic catalog of the most-performed songs in the Christian music world. In 1993, he composed "I Am Redeemed," which stayed in the top-ten music charts for five years! He holds his audiences spellbound as he sings his award-winning songs. His compositions have been recorded by Bill Gaither, Amy Grant, Natalie Cole, Diana Ross, and Point of Grace, some of the biggest names in popular music. An ordained minister, he has appeared in major venues and on television shows around the world.

WHEN I WAS A CHILD, our Christmas evenings were spent at a special church service. The church encouraged each family to come and give testimony. Every year, the children's choir would sing Christmas carols. Mother was all about me singing in the children's Little Sunbeams Choir. I wasn't real crazy about it, but *wow*, was Ms. Martha Campbell, the choir instructor, real pretty! The other kids teased me 'cause I did every-thing she asked—they knew I had a crush on her. She had such an influence on my whole family. She inspired my singing and was a mentor to all the children of the church.

I remember one particular Christmas very well. Ms. Martha read the Christmas story, and then the kids sang the finale, "The First Noel." I didn't know Ms. Martha was going to ask me to sing the lead, and I certainly didn't realize how much that night would direct the rest of my life. It really was my first big moment in singing. I sang one verse and said, "That's all I'm singing." I looked over at my mother and saw she was not happy with me at all. Everyone else was laughing, but not Mother. She said, "That was your big moment and you stopped the song." I learned a valuable lesson and ever since, never stopped singing!

Today, "The First Noel" is one of the first Christmas songs I sing on my Christmas tours wherever I am during the holiday season. As an adult I realize how fortunate I have been to have such great holiday memories, and it is a pleasure to be able to keep singing. I never want to stop.

Redeemed Pork Chops with Collard Green Casserole

I had a friend who used to visit me here in Chicago every summer. She would always cook me her famous pork chops. I loved them. She shared her secret with me, and so I am sharing it with you. Believe me, these are the best pork chops you'll ever eat! Serve the chops with your favorite veggies or the Collard Green Casserole and the end result will be a perfect meal! *Serves 8*

Casserole

1 (10-ounce) package smoked turkey pieces
1 large bunch collard greens (about 2 pounds)
Salt and cracked black pepper, to taste
1 cup diced cooked ham
1 large onion, chopped
1 (16-ounce) can diced tomatoes
2 (7-ounce) packages cornbread mix

1 cup shredded reduced-fat cheese, such as Cheddar, if desired

Pork Chops

8 pork chops
Salt and cracked black pepper, to taste
1 cup unbleached, all-purpose flour
$1/2$ cup Dijon mustard
$1/4$ cup vegetable oil

1. To make the casserole: Place the turkey in a soup pot along with 5 cups of water. Bring the mixture to a boil, reduce the heat to low, and simmer for 30 minutes. Coarsely chop the collard greens and add to the turkey. Bring the mixture to a boil, reduce the heat to low, and simmer for $1 1/2$ hours. Drain the greens, saving the broth and turkey pieces for another use.

2. Preheat the oven to 400°F.

3. Arrange the greens evenly across the bottom of a 13 by 9-inch baking dish. Season the collards with several pinches of salt and pepper, or to taste. Scat-ter the ham over the greens, followed by the onion and tomatoes.

4. Combine both cornbread mixes in a large bowl and prepare the batter according to the package directions. Using a spatula, spread the cornbread batter evenly over the collard mixture. Sprinkle the shredded cheese, if using, over the batter. Bake the casserole for 30 minutes or until the cornbread is cooked through.

5. To prepare the pork chops: Season both sides of each pork chop with salt and pepper to taste. Place the flour on a large plate and season with salt and pepper. Coat both sides of each pork chop with 1 tablespoon of mustard, then dredge in the flour.

6. Working in batches, heat 2 tablespoons of the oil in a large nonstick skillet over medium heat. When hot, add 4 of the pork chops and cook for 4 to 5 minutes on each side or until the meat is just cooked through. Repeat the process with the remaining oil and pork chops.

Ronnie Milsap

RONNIE MILSAP has had a mind-boggling career. He has won six Grammys, six *Billboard* awards, eight Country Music Association awards, three Academy of Country Music awards, and four *Cash Box* awards. He has had an astounding forty number-one singles and has sold more than twenty-three million records. While Ronnie is notably recognized as a singer of country music, he has always loved delving into other styles of music, sometimes singing rhythm and blues or a pop song from time to time. He's even performed the standards of George and Ira Gershwin, Rodgers and Hart, and Cole Porter.

Ronnie with his wife, Joyce, and his son, Todd

DURING THE HOLIDAYS, we visit the neighbors and exchange gifts with them. It is such a wonderful celebration because we have so many decorations on our gates and our house. On Christmas Eve, our families arrive. The nieces and nephews are all over the house; and because it is all about the children, we have gifts for them. For the adults, that night is all about giving gifts and not about receiving.

Christmas morning with my wife, Joyce, our son, Todd, and our three grandchildren is a very exciting time. I have the videocamera, a couple of grand pianos, and the big Christmas tree all set up in the living room where we open presents and make a big mess. All the while, we enjoy the sounds of the music of Perry Como, The Carpenters, and Bobby Vinton, along with the instrumental music I love. My favorite song to sing is "O Holy Night." I can remember singing it in the chorus when I was in school.

What a Difference You Make Breakfast Strata

What's a Christmas morning without this staple casserole? It's an extra special way to bring the holiday into your dining room. Serves 8 to 10

1 pound sausage meat, casings removed

6 slices white sandwich bread, toasted and cubed

1 cup grated Cheddar cheese

8 large eggs

2 cups milk

1 teaspoon dry mustard

1 teaspoon salt

1. Place a large nonstick skillet over medium heat. Add the sausage meat to the dry skillet and sauté until browned and crumbled. Drain off any excess fat.

2. Arrange the toasted bread cubes in an even layer across the bottom of a 13 by 9-inch baking dish. Scatter the browned sausage over the bread. Sprinkle on the cheese.

3. Blend the eggs with the milk, dry mustard, and salt in a large bowl. Pour over the bread and sausage mixture. Seal the dish with aluminum foil, and refrigerate for at least 8 hours.

4. When ready to serve, preheat the oven to 350°F. Keeping the aluminum foil on the baking dish, bake the strata for 40 minutes. Remove the foil and cook for 12 minutes more, or until the top is golden.

Barbara Mandrell

ITH A CAREER in recording and television that has spanned more than thirty years, Barbara Mandrell is one of America's most popular performers and has received over seventy-five major awards. She has released more than thirty albums, featuring many songs that climbed high on the country and pop charts. She starred in her own highly rated variety show, and her 1990 autobiography, *Get to the Heart of My Story,* made the *New York Times* best-seller list and became a made-for-television movie. As an actress, she has appeared on many television shows, including *Touched by an Angel; Baywatch; Dr. Quinn, Medicine Woman; Diagnosis Murder;* and *Love Boat.* Barbara is a true star in every sense of the word.

Barbara Mandrell with her husband, Ken Dudney, and
children Jaime, Nathan, and Matthew

AS KIDS, we were not the up-at-the-crack-of-dawn, run-straight-to-the-Christmas-tree type family. Instead we sat down and ate doughnuts or cinnamon rolls that were waiting for us. Then we opened our Christmas presents around the tree, everyone taking a turn, one present at a time. Even the dogs had presents, and they knew which ones were theirs by the smells.

We spend many Christmases in Aspen because we are guaranteed snow, and we all love to ski. One year we cooked a turkey in our cabin, which was at a very high elevation, so we knew it would take longer to cook. But that turkey began to smell horrible, and it tasted even worse. We had to throw the whole bird out. My husband, Ken, jumped in the car, drove down to the village, and found a store that was open. Ken bought a roasted chicken that was as good as any turkey. That was the day Ken saved Christmas dinner.

There is something else that is very special for me on Christmas. I was born on December 25, and each year we celebrate my birthday after our Christmas dinner. I wanted my birthday presents to be separate from the Christmas presents, so they are wrapped in birthday paper. I feel blessed to share the birthday of our Savior Jesus Christ.

Do-Right, Outta Sight Christmas Turkey

No matter where we are on Christmas and what else we have, we can be sure there will be a turkey on our Christmas dinner table. And if you enjoy turkey as much as we do, then I know you'll enjoy this recipe for our family's traditional Christmas turkey. **Serves 12 or more**

1 (18-pound) turkey, giblets removed
3 tablespoons olive oil
2 lemons

$1/2$ **cup fresh oregano leaves (stripped off several sprigs)**
$1/2$ **cup fresh thyme leaves (stripped off several sprigs)**
$1/2$ **cup fresh rosemary needles (stripped off several sprigs)**
$1/2$ **cup torn fresh basil leaves**
$1/2$ **pound (2 sticks) unsalted butter, cut into pieces**
2 garlic cloves, minced
1 tablespoon paprika
Salt and cracked black pepper, to taste

1. Preheat the oven to 350°F. Line a roasting pan (that is at least 4 inches deep) with enough aluminum foil so that the excess foil from the sides and short ends of the roasting pan can be tented over the bird to completely seal it.

2. Rinse the turkey under cold water and pat dry. Using your hands, carefully separate the skin from the breast meat. Do not remove the skin, just pull it away from the meat to form a pocket. Place the turkey in the prepared pan. Rub the breast meat with 1 tablespoon of the olive oil. Cut the lemons in half and squeeze the juice from both lemons over the breast meat. Place the juiced halves in the cavity of the bird.

3. Sprinkle half of the oregano, thyme, rosemary, and basil leaves over the breast meat. Place the remaining herbs in the cavity of the bird, along with the butter and garlic.

4. Rub the remaining 2 tablespoons of olive oil over the skin of the entire bird and then sprinkle with the paprika and a generous amount of salt and pepper. Fill the roasting pan with enough water so that it measures 2 inches deep around the bird. Pull the foil up over the bird and loosely crimp it to seal—you will be opening the foil several times to baste. Roast the turkey, basting every 30 minutes or so, for $3^1/2$ to 4 hours, or until an instant-read thermometer reads 165°F when inserted mid-thigh. Remove the foil for the last 10 minutes of cooking. Serve with the pan juices (or use them to make a gravy).

Tim McGraw

TIM MCGRAW is enjoying a remarkable career. His nine albums spawned twenty-three number-one singles and sold thirty-two million copies. Tim's sell-out tours consistently rank near the top in financial and entertainment terms and his scores of honors and awards— like the 2001 Entertainer of the Year, a Grammy, and a 2004 People's Choice Award for favorite male musical performer—have made him one of America's biggest stars. His hits, too numerous to mention, continue to flow, causing his star to shine much brighter with every release. Tim is married to the beautiful superstar singer Faith Hill. They live in Nashville, Tennessee, with their three daughters. Their lives are full. Their careers flourish.

I LOVE CHRISTMAS. It is the most special time of the year. And let me tell you, having an Italian mother made it even more special.

Mom would make her recipe for lasagna or spaghetti on Christmas Eve. The table would be set real fancy and festive. We all had wine with our meal. Even us kids, just like a real Italian family. For dessert Mom always fixed her scrumptious fruit parfaits and my favorite yellow cake with chocolate frosting. We even made cookies, but not just for us. We always left a plate full of cookies and a glass of milk for the special visitor who would be dropping by later that night. Even as we grew older, we still left them out. Momma still loves to share her favorite holiday memory of my childhood friend Lance and the Christmas cookies for Santa. Momma recalls Lance asking me, "Do ya'll still believe in Santa?" I replied with a whisper, "Momma does, and Momma says once you stop believing in him, he stops coming." So, cookies and milk are always left out at my house because Santa is coming to town on Christmas Eve.

Faith and I still continue those family Christmas traditions, and we've added some of our own. We began a new tradition two years ago on our daughter Audrey's birthday, December 6. That is when we put up our Christmas tree and decorate it. That day has only grown in joy as the years pass. We also enjoy Christmas day a bit differently now. We buy new pj's for everyone and we wear them all day.

Momma Betty's Italian Lasagna

Mom made her special recipe for lasagna on Christmas. I love this great dish so much. All I can say is I always want some more of it! And you will too. Serves 10 to 12

2 tablespoons olive oil

3 pounds ground sirloin

2 pounds (small slab) pork ribs

1 pound Italian sausages, casings removed

6 cups tomato sauce

2 cups canned whole tomatoes

1 cup tomato paste

1/2 cup sliced mushrooms

3 garlic cloves, minced

1 small onion, chopped

3 tablespoons chopped fresh basil

2 tablespoons chopped fresh oregano

$\frac{1}{2}$ teaspoon sugar

2 (16-ounce) boxes lasagna noodles

1 pound ricotta cheese

1 cup shredded mozzarella cheese

1 cup shredded provolone cheese

1 cup grated Parmesan cheese

1 cup grated Romano cheese

1. Place 1 tablespoon of the oil in a large skillet over medium heat. When hot, add the sirloin and sauté until browned and crumbled. Drain off any excess fat. Transfer the meat to a soup pot.

2. Add the remaining 1 tablespoon of oil to the same skillet. Add the pork ribs and sausage and cook until the meat is brown and the sausage is crumbled. Drain off any excess fat and transfer the ribs and sausage to the soup pot with the sirloin.

3. Add 1 cup of water to the soup pot, along with the tomato sauce, whole tomatoes, tomato paste, mushrooms, garlic, onion, basil, oregano, and

sugar. Bring the mixture to a boil. Reduce the heat to very low and gently simmer the sauce, stirring occasionally, for 7 hours. Remove the rib bones from the sauce.

4. Bring a large pot of water to a boil for cooking the pasta. Working in batches, cook each box of lasagna noodles, according to the package directions, until al dente. Drain and rinse under cold water.

5. Preheat the oven to 350°F.

6. Using two 13 by 9-inch baking dishes, spread a ladleful of the tomato sauce evenly across the bottom of each baking dish. Cover the sauce with a layer of lasagna noodles, some of the meat sauce, a few dollops of ricotta cheese, and a sprinkling of the mozzarella, provolone, Parmesan, and Romano cheeses. Continue layering the lasagnas in this manner, ending with a final layer of the four cheeses for both lasagnas. Bake the lasagnas for 30 minutes, or until hot all the way through.

Tim McGraw with his sisters, Sandy and Tracey, and his mother, Betty (middle)

John Michael Montgomery

OHN MICHAEL MONTGOMERY says that good songs are the reason he is able to return to the top of the charts over and over. His uncanny ability to find the right songs and perform them to everyone's satisfaction has driven a twelve-year career that has produced hits such as "Letters from Home," "The Little Girl," "I Swear," and "I Can Love You Like That." His continuing stream of hits has permanently established a place for him in country music. John Michael resides in Kentucky with his wife, Crystal, and their two children, Madison and Walker.

WHEN THE TOUR SEASON slows down, I am glad to have valuable time to spend with my family over the holiday season. I love to hunt, and the winter weather is perfect for hunting on my farm. My wife's parents, Carl and Carol, come over on Christmas Eve and I cook for the entire family. We gather around the table and enjoy my special dishes. Even my kids, Madison and Walker, look forward to Daddy's Christmas dinner. A home-cooked meal with meat I have hunted myself—well, that's a Montgomery tradition.

Wild Goose with Currant Sauce

Slow baking with just the right combination of flavors cooks up the kind of meal I really love. I hope you enjoy my recipe. **Serves 8 to 10**

Geese

2 (8- to 10-pound) geese
6 pitted prunes, chopped
1 large orange, unpeeled, cut into wedges
1 sweet-tart apple, cored and cut into wedges
2 (6-ounce) packages onion soup mix
2 cups dry red wine
2 commercial cooking bags, each large enough to
    hold a turkey

Currant Sauce

1/4 cup dry port
1/4 cup Worcestershire sauce
1/4 cup ketchup
1/4 cup red currant jelly
2 tablespoons unsalted butter

1. Preheat the oven to 350°F.

2. **To make the geese:** Remove any excess fat, rinse, and pat the birds dry. Combine the prunes with the orange and apple in a small bowl; toss to mix. Place half of the fruit in one goose cavity and the remaining fruit in the other bird's cavity.

3. Place the onion soup mix and the red wine in a medium bowl. Add 2 cups of water and whisk until the soup mix has dissolved. Place each goose, breast side up, in its cooking bag. Place the bags in a large roasting pan and pour half of the red wine mixture into each bag. Seal the bags according to package directions, and cut six very small slits into the top of each bag to let some of the steam escape. Bake the birds for 3 1/2 hours, or until an instant-read thermometer inserted in the bird's thigh reads 165°F. Let the geese cool slightly before removing from their bags. Carve the birds and serve with the bag juices, fruit, and currant sauce.

4. **To make the currant sauce:** Place the port, Worcestershire, ketchup, currant jelly, and butter in a small saucepan over low heat. Stir until the mixture begins to bubble. Transfer to a serving bowl with a spoon and serve with the birds.

Wayne Newton

JUST SAY "Mr. Las Vegas" when you are referring to Wayne Newton and you have said enough. Everyone knows you are talking about one of the greatest entertainers of our time. From the age of six, Wayne has made sure he doesn't leave the stage until the audience has its money's worth. He has appeared live in front of more than thirty million people. He has established himself in movies and television, appearing with such greats as Jackie Gleason, Lucille Ball, and Jack Benny. He appears frequently on the talk shows and is one of the most widely acclaimed and honored entertainers in history.

To date, Wayne has recorded 148 albums and has had numerous hits, including "Danke Schoen," "Dreams of the Everyday Housewife," and "Daddy, Don't You Walk So Fast." Wayne says, "I want to be a man who dares to dream and pursue it, using my head for myself and my heart for others, to leave the world a better place than I found it." Mission accomplished.

Told by Martha Bolton, former writer for Bob Hope's and Wayne Newton's USO tours

THE VOICE on the other end of the line was unmistakably Wayne Newton's. He was calling to ask if I would be interested in writing some material for a holiday show that he was putting together for our men and women serving in the armed forces. The year was 2001 and Wayne had just been selected as the new chairman of the USO Celebrity Circle. He would soon be embarking on his first USO tour in that role.

And Wayne was doing it right, too. Following in the footsteps of Bob Hope, Wayne was determined to take the best show possible to our dedicated soldiers. His lineup of celebrities was going to include Jessica Simpson, the Dallas Cowboys cheerleaders, Bo Derek, Miss USA Kandace Krueger, Ruth Pointer of the Pointer Sisters, *Ally McBeal*'s Peter MacNicol, country-and-western singer Neil McCoy, comedian Rob Schneider, and the popular reggae-pop singer Shaggy. It was an all-star lineup to be sure, headed by entertainer extraordinaire himself, Wayne Newton.

A talented writer-performer, he and his gifted cast of celebrities surprised no one when they delivered a show that the soldiers thoroughly enjoyed and would not soon forget. The tour included stops in Bosnia, Budapest, Naples, Vicenza, and Aviano.

Wayne has faithfully continued to bring the spirit of Christmas to our men and women of the armed forces every year since. Like Bob Hope's tours, it is a mission of the heart. But instead of Bob's "Thanks for the Memory," Wayne closes his shows with his own signature song, "Danke Schoen." It's his own personal thank-you to the troops.

Mr. Las Vegas Coconut Chicken

One of the best chicken dishes I've ever tasted. It's amazing what a little coconut can do. Serves 4

Chicken

2 pounds skinless, boneless chicken breasts
Salt and cracked black pepper, to taste
1 cup sweetened shredded coconut
$1/2$ cup dry bread crumbs
$1/2$ cup unbleached, all-purpose flour
$2/3$ cup alcohol-free prepared piña colada mix
   (available at supermarkets)
2 large eggs
1 cup vegetable oil

Sauce

$2^1/2$ teaspoons vegetable oil
1 red bell pepper, stemmed, cored, and diced
2 garlic cloves, minced
1 cup chicken broth
$1/3$ cup sugar
$1/3$ cup unsweetened coconut milk
1 orange, juiced, rind reserved

1 lemon, juiced, rind reserved
1 tablespoon cornstarch
Salt and cracked black pepper, to taste

1. To make the chicken: Cut each breast into 1-inch-wide strips and season with salt and pepper to taste.

2. Combine the coconut and bread crumbs in a shallow dish and toss to mix. Place the flour on a large plate.

3. Place the piña colada mix and the eggs in a bowl and whisk to combine.

4. Heat the oil in a large skillet over medium heat until it reaches 350°F. Test the oil by dropping in a small piece of fresh bread. If the bread rises and immediately turns golden, then the oil is hot enough.

5. Dredge each strip of chicken in flour, dip it in the egg mixture, and then roll in the coconut mixture. Working in batches, fry several pieces of chicken at a time, until golden and cooked through. Drain on a wire rack lined with a double layer of paper towels.

6. To make the sauce: Heat the oil in a medium shallow saucepan over medium heat. Add the bell pepper and garlic and sauté for 5 minutes. Stir in the chicken broth, sugar, and coconut milk. Add the juice from the orange and lemon to the sauce. Quarter the citrus rinds and add to the sauce. Bring the sauce to a boil, reduce the heat to low, and simmer for 15 minutes. Using a slotted spoon, remove each rind wedge, gently pressing on each one to remove any sauce, and discard. Simmer the sauce for another 10 minutes.

7. Combine the cornstarch with 1 tablespoon of cold water in a small bowl. Whisk into the sauce and stir until thickened. Season with salt and pepper to taste. To serve, arrange the chicken pieces on 4 serving plates and top with the sauce.

William Lee Golden

IN A CROWD, in a photo, or on a stage, you can't miss William Lee Golden. His recognizable long hair and beard set him apart from everyone else. William Lee, a farmer's son who didn't experience the luxury of electricity until he was eight years old, transcended his poor beginnings in Brewton, Alabama, to become one of America's most beloved entertainers. In 1965, William Lee moved to Nashville and filled the baritone position with the Oak Ridge Boys. The Oaks decided to try the country scene and hit immediately with "Ya'll Come Back Saloon," followed by one of the biggest records in history, "Elvira." The Oak Ridge Boys have recorded a long string of hits that have dominated the charts for years.

Solomon, Brenda, and William Lee Golden

A GOLDEN CHRISTMAS is filled with family traditions. It starts on Christmas Eve morning at Golden Era Plantation. Built in 1786, Golden Era is the oldest brick home in the state of Tennessee, and it's the place my wife, Brenda; youngest son, Solomon; and I call home. My older three sons, Rusty, Craig, and Chris, and their families congregate at our home in the morning, along with a longtime friend of mine, Richard Brown, who comes to our home every Thanksgiving and Christmas. While we usually have a formal, intimate dinner on Christmas night with a few close friends, this family gathering is brunch—buffet-style. There is something for everyone: blueberry pancakes, casseroles, desserts, and a family favorite: grape and pineapple ham, which I bake and contribute to the spread.

After our stomachs are full and our belts are loosened, we gather in our study where our tree is decorated with ornaments we have collected from our travels. In every city or country we visit, my wife buys an ornament for the tree to remember our journeys. Having very talented children and grandchildren, we turn on the microphones and take turns singing holiday and gospel songs. Someone always breaks out a few of my mother's poems and reads them aloud. Every year the youngest child who knows how to read recites the story of Jesus' birth, found in the second chapter of the Book of Luke. This is our way of keeping Christ in Christmas. After the reading, we pass out the presents and paper starts to fly like Rudolph across the room. In between helping put together toys and looking for batteries, we sit around enjoying each other's company and reflecting on our past year and our hopes for the next.

Down Home Sweet Gaggie's Chicken Casserole

When you are on the road a lot and grabbing your meals as you go, good home cooking is something you miss. My mom, whom we call Gaggie, cooks the best chicken casserole. Anytime of the year I get to enjoy it is a holiday, but the holidays are even more special with that extra touch of a mother's love. Serves 4

1 pound Ritz crackers (4 sleeves)
1 cup diced cooked chicken
1 (8-ounce) can sliced water chestnuts, drained
1 (10$\frac{1}{2}$-ounce) can cream of mushroom soup
1 (10$\frac{1}{2}$-ounce) can cream of chicken soup
$\frac{1}{2}$ cup sour cream
1 teaspoon dried basil
Salt and cracked black pepper, to taste

1. Preheat the oven to 350°F.

2. Crush the crackers and set aside 2 cups of the cracker crumbs. Sprinkle the remaining cracker crumbs across the bottom of a 13 by 9-inch baking dish. Scatter the chicken over the crumbs and top with the water chestnuts.

3. Place the cream of mushroom and cream of chicken soups in a medium bowl. Whisk in the sour cream and basil; season with salt and pepper to taste. Pour over the chicken mixture, then top with the reserved cracker crumbs. Bake for 20 minutes or until bubbly and golden.

Tim Rushlow

IM RUSHLOW began his professional career as lead singer of a contemporary country band, Little Texas. After leaving the band, he joined Atlantic Records in the spring of 1999 as a solo artist and released his debut album, *Tim Rushlow*. When Atlantic Records closed its Nashville operation, Tim decided to put together a group of talented musicians and become the band RUSHLOW. Tim says, "I don't want to win the Nobel Peace Prize. I just want to be a great artist who can make great music that is going to make a difference."

Tim Rushlow with his band on the USO tour

MY BEST CHRISTMAS happened in 2003 when my band, RUSHLOW, and I traveled overseas to entertain our troops for the holidays. Music is a way to touch one's soul, even more so during wartime. We saw how quickly music affected people and how sweet it is to see a soldier travel in his mind to a sweeter place through the lyrics and melody of a song.

We took this trip for one reason. We wanted to say thank you for the gift of being able to make our music any way we see fit in a free country. We did eleven shows in eighteen days and had been to fourteen countries by the time we got home.

Christmas Eve we were at the secured port in Dubai, UAE [United Arab Emirates], doing a show for the navy and a full fleet of ships. The sun went down as we all sang "O Holy Night," and one single northern star appeared. Only God could give a gift that large. There was silence after the song and then thundering applause with tears.

I realized, after making three stops on three continents to make it home Christmas night to be with my wife and daughters, that the best gift was to once again stand on free soil with my family. I'll never forget the first-class treatment extended to us by the navy, and I will go to play music for the troops whenever I am asked. It is the least I can do. Merry Christmas!

Speechless Venison with Blueberry Sauce

Every Christmas we have several great cooking evenings, but my family's favorite is my blueberry venison tenderloins. Venison is hard to get unless you hunt, like I do. And even then, the tenderloins don't last long. This is one of our favorites. I usually serve these with broccoli sautéed with garlic and a little orange juice and olive oil, sweet potatoes, and a fresh salad. A good Cabernet always works well, too. Enjoy! Serves 4

> 4 (4-ounce) venison steaks
> Salt and cracked black pepper, to taste
> 2 tablespoons packed light brown sugar
> 2 tablespoons malt vinegar
> 1½ cups fresh (or frozen) blueberries
> ¼ cup dry white wine
> ¼ cup Dubonnet rouge
> 1 tablespoon olive oil
> 1½ teaspoons cornstarch

1. Season the venison steaks on both sides with salt and pepper to taste. Set aside.

2. Combine the sugar and vinegar in a small saucepan over low heat. Stir until the sugar has dissolved. Add the blueberries, wine, and Dubonnet and simmer over low heat for 10 minutes.

3. Place a large nonstick skillet over high heat. Add the oil. When hot, add the venison steaks and cook for 1 to 2 minutes on each side, or until medium rare. (Venison is extremely lean and cooks quickly.)

4. Blend together the cornstarch with 1 tablespoon of water in a small bowl. Whisk into the blueberry sauce and cook over low heat until the sauce has thickened.

5. To serve, cut each venison steak into thin slices and fan on a serving plate. Spoon the blueberry sauce over the meat.

Jerry Schilling

$\mathcal{J}$ERRY SCHILLING'S long and productive career started in 1964, when at the age of twenty-one he was hired by Elvis Presley. Boyhood friends since 1954, Elvis brought Jerry to Los Angeles as his personal aide. He started as Elvis's movie stand-in and learned Hollywood from the ground up, branching out into the areas of public relations, film editing, and producing. In 1975, he formed Jerry Schilling Management and was soon directing the careers of Jerry Lee Lewis, The Sweet Inspirations, Peter Noone of Herman's Hermits, Lisa Marie Presley, and The Beach Boys. His long and close association with Elvis led to numerous production credits on feature films, television series, prime-time specials, radio, and video.

Jerry Schilling with Elvis Presley

I KNEW ELVIS ten years before I went to work with him, the same week he recorded his first record. We used to play touch football on Sundays. He wasn't popular then, but I thought he was pretty cool, and I think he remembered that.

In 1964, I went to work for Elvis. I can remember that first Christmas spent at Graceland, a very warm and exciting time filled with much anticipation. Before I even reached the front door, I felt the Christmas spirit as I turned into the driveway and saw the beautiful lights adorning the trees, and the life-size manger scene.

He was a much better giver than a receiver, so his father would bring a list of about fifty charities and Elvis would write the checks to each one. He wanted to touch all faiths during the holiday season, and it was a universal and very diversified effort.

Christmas dinner at Graceland was not really different from the meals we had on other days. It wasn't easy to sit down at a table for a meal because there were so many people coming in and out. Elvis normally wanted meatloaf or pot roast, but the cooks usually made a fancier dessert at Christmastime. My favorite was fresh, homemade banana pudding.

Christmas holidays for my wife and me are even more special because we are still part of the Presley family. We join Priscilla and Lisa with their families at Lake Arrowhead for a formal dinner. I now have more treasured Presley Christmas memories.

Southern-Style Heartbreak Pot Roast

Warm up your heart with a favorite from Graceland. Elvis loved his pot roast and the cooks at Graceland knew how to cook it just right. May I suggest you follow it up with a big pan of fresh banana pudding? A feast fit for a king . . . like Elvis! Serves 6

1 (3-pound) chuck roast
Salt and cracked black pepper, to taste
1 cup unbleached, all-purpose flour
2 tablespoons vegetable oil
1 (6-ounce) package onion soup mix
1 (10$\frac{1}{2}$-ounce) can golden mushroom soup
4 medium boiling potatoes, sliced
4 carrots, peeled and cut into chunks
2 medium onions, cut into wedges

1. Preheat the oven to 350°F.

2. Season the beef on all sides with salt and pepper to taste. Place the flour in a large baking dish and dredge the beef in the flour.

3. Heat the oil in a 4-quart Dutch oven over medium heat. Add the meat and cook on all sides until nicely browned.

4. Combine the onion soup mix and the mushroom soup in a medium bowl. Using the mushroom soup can as a measure, add 2 cans of water (21 ounces) to the bowl. Stir the mixture and then pour over the meat. Bake the meat, covered, for 1 hour. Add the potatoes, carrots, and onions and a little more water if the sauce appears too thick, cover, and bake for 45 minutes more or until the meat is tender and cooked through.

Lance Smith

*A*FTER ACHIEVING SUCCESS on the Nashville music video scene, Lance Smith moved to Los Angeles in 1999 to try his hand at acting. For a while, he worked on various sitcoms and other programs. His first major break came when he signed a deal to tour with the Dixie Chicks. He instantly became an audience favorite with his unique blend of humor and personality. His ninety-city, nationwide tour prepared him for something even greater. Country Music Television (CMT) held a nationwide search for an on-air host. His prior success in music videos and time spent on sound stages in Hollywood helped him become CMT's first VJ in the network's history.

Lance Smith as a child, with his parents

THOUGH ALMOST ALL of my childhood and young adult life was spent living in the South, two years were spent in Hawaii. It was the end of fall when we moved. And though it was just a simple job transfer for my father, as an eight-year-old I was leaving my world behind. Friends, extended family, even the rolling landscape to which I was so accustomed would be just a memory for the upcoming Christmas holiday. What about the Christmas tree? What about Santa? Would he know where to find us? And most important, what about snow?! I was smart enough to know where Hawaii sat on the globe, and even then I knew Jack Frost didn't cruise by that way.

The first few weeks were the hardest. For a child in a new school, making friends can sometimes be difficult, especially with the culture shock I was going through. But the adjustments were made and Christmas arrived. Though the streets were absent of snow, the tree was there, Santa found our house, and I was with my family. It was the first time in my life that I truly understood the relationship between family and Christmas. I don't remember one single present that year. I only remember the love of my family and how beautiful the water looked as we spent Christmas Day on the beach. *Mele kalikimaka* to you, Santa Claus.

Holiday Island Chicken and Rice

As a child, I spent two years living in Hawaii, and I can't help considering this a must on our menu. It's a happy holiday addition to the veggies and desserts that grace the Christmas table. Santa Claus won't mind taking a few extra minutes at your house if he gets a taste of this dish. Serves 4

1 (20-ounce) can pineapple chunks with juice
$^1/_2$ cup raisins
$^1/_2$ cup sliced scallions
1 garlic clove, minced
$^1/_2$ teaspoon ground ginger
2 tablespoons soy sauce
3 cups cooked white or brown rice
2 cups cooked diced chicken or ham
2 tablespoons sweetened shredded coconut

1. Saving the juice, drain the pineapple chunks. Place 2$^1/_2$ tablespoons of the reserved pineapple juice in a large nonstick skillet over medium heat. Add the raisins, scallions, garlic, and ginger and simmer for 3 minutes. Stir in the soy sauce.

2. Add the cooked rice and chicken, along with the pineapple chunks and 2 tablespoons more of the reserved pineapple juice. Stir to blend. Cover the skillet, reduce the heat to low, and simmer for 5 minutes. Garnish the dish with the coconut and serve.

Jett Williams

JETT WILLIAMS has a story to tell that would make a great movie. In 1953, she was born into fame that she didn't legally receive until 1987, when the courts declared her to be the biological daughter of the great Hank Williams Sr. Relinquished by her natural mother, baby Bobbie Jett of Nashville was taken into the home of Hank's mother, Lillian, who adopted her. Unfortunately, Lillian passed away two months after the adoption was final. Jett was two years old at the time. The Williams family no longer wanted the child, so she became a ward of the state of Alabama and was placed in a foster home at the age of three. Since achieving her rightful place in society, her inherited talent has helped her establish her well-deserved place in country music.

Jett Williams and her husband, Keith

MY DADDY, Hank Williams Sr., died before I was born. I lived with my grandmother (his mother) until she passed away when I was two years old. I was made a ward of the state of Alabama and stayed in foster homes until I was adopted at around six or seven years of age. My family lived in Mobile, Alabama, on the Gulf Coast; and Christmas there wasn't cold like I used to see in the Christmas books and movies with snow and horses and sleighs. On the Gulf Coast, you are looking at crabs and sand. There were a lot of pine trees in that area, which wasn't as developed as it is now, and we would go out into the fields and cut down a tree every year for our Christmas tree. I still have some of the fragile blue and green balls that we used to decorate those trees.

Today, before we go to midnight Christmas Mass, my husband, Keith, and I sit down by our Christmas tree and read each other our favorite Christmas stories from Christmas books we have collected over the years. Keith even has a copy of 'Twas the Night before Christmas from the first year it was published. Our Christmas dinner is very traditional—turkey, dressing, and all the fixings right down to the cranberry sauce. I still cut down my Christmas trees each year and share pies, cakes, and candies with our neighbors.

I want the children of St. Jude and everyone else to remember the lights on the Christmas tree. Even though we see them only at Christmastime, you can close your eyes any time and imagine the most beautifully lit Christmas tree, the star on the top, and the magic of this wonderful season. Hope is our foundation!

Hank's Baby Girl Sweet Ham Alabama Casserole

Turkey, dressing, and all the traditional fixin's are great, but you'll be glad you added this ham casserole delight. We live on a farm in the country, and we like to share our favorite foods with our neighbors. We'll bring the ham casserole, and you bring the pie. We'll sit down and share a meal and good conversation. Serves 6

> 1½ pounds cooked ham
> 1½ pounds uncooked ground pork
> 1½ cups dry bread crumbs
> 2 large eggs
> 1¼ cups milk
> 1¼ cups firmly packed light brown sugar
> ½ cup cider vinegar
> 1 tablespoon Dijon mustard

1. Preheat the oven to 350°F.

2. Using a meat grinder or food processor, grind or process the cooked ham until well ground. Transfer to a large bowl and add the ground pork, bread crumbs, eggs, and milk. Stir well to blend. Form the mixture into a loaf-shaped mound, and place, rounded side up, in an 11 by 7-inch baking dish. Bake for 45 minutes.

3. Combine the sugar, vinegar, mustard, and ¼ cup of water in a small saucepan. Bring the mixture to a boil, reduce the heat to low, and simmer, stirring often, for 5 minutes. Pour the sauce over the loaf and bake for 45 minutes more.

Alan and Denise Jackson

MULTITALENTED SINGER-SONGWRITER Alan Jackson moved to Nashville, Tennessee, from his hometown of Newnan, Georgia, in 1985. He soon signed as a songwriter with Glen Campbell's music publishing company and later inked a deal with Arista Records as its first country artist. From his first single, "Blue-Blooded Woman," which peaked at a disappointing number forty-five on the country charts in 1989, Alan has gone on to sell more than forty-three million albums. He has scored more than thirty number-one singles, twenty-one of which he wrote or co-wrote. Always true to his country style, he continues his string of hits with every release.

ALAN AND I grew up in Newnan, Georgia. I met Alan at the local hangout, the Dairy Queen, when he was seventeen and I was sixteen. We didn't start dating until after Alan graduated high school. We seem to have been made for each other. We dated for three and a half years before we knew we never wanted to part. We married when Alan was twenty-one and I was just nineteen. Surpassing all odds, we have spent twenty-five years together.

We have three precious and beautiful daughters, Mattie, Ali, and Dani. While our girls are sleeping (or pretending to), Alan and I get ready for Santa.

Alan and Denise Jackson with Mattie, Ali, and Dani

The last thing to be set up is our videocamera. Even though the girls might get up early, they cannot go downstairs until the camera is rolling to catch the excitement and happiness they express as they hurry down the stairs and go to the presents around our big family tree in the living room. They first see what Santa has brought. Then they open presents while munching on sausage balls. When lunchtime comes everyone is ready for our Christmas feast of ham, turkey, cornbread dressing, corn, green beans, sweet potato soufflé, Alan's mother Ruth's lime salad, yeast rolls, and desserts like red velvet cake and chocolate cheesecake.

We have several Christmas trees decorated around the house, but there is only one family tree. This tree is among our strongest family traditions. It is filled with ornaments that are old and very sentimental. Some ornaments our girls have made. Some ornaments Alan made back when he was in the Boy Scouts. We even have ornaments that we bought for our very first Christmas together in 1979. Some have been taped and glued through the years to keep them together, but they all are special and each has a story. The tree represents our family as we grow from year to year. Christmas is such a great time to reflect on our family and the many blessings we have been given. Merry Christmas everyone!

Chattahoochee Cornbread and Cornbread Dressing

The smell of cornbread baking in the oven brings with it a welcome, down-home feeling. And this cornbread dressing is the best one around. Just add it to your Christmas dinner along with all the fixin's. It's always a hit at our house. Serves 6

Cornbread

1 tablespoon vegetable oil
1 cup self-rising cornmeal
2 tablespoons self-rising flour
3/4 cup buttermilk

Dressing

1 1/2 cups crumbled white biscuits, or small cubes of white sandwich-style bread
1 medium onion, chopped
4 cups chicken broth
8 tablespoons (1 stick) margarine
2 large eggs
Salt and cracked black pepper, to taste

1. To make the cornbread: Preheat the oven to 450°F. Coat a 6-inch round ovenproof skillet (or comparable size baking pan) with the oil.

2. Whisk together the cornmeal and flour in a medium bowl. Add the buttermilk and stir to blend. Transfer the batter to the oiled skillet and bake for 20 minutes, or until a wooden skewer inserted into the center of the bread comes out clean. Let cool for several minutes before turning out onto a wire rack to cool completely.

3. To make the dressing: Grease a 13 by 9-inch baking dish.

4. Crumble the cornbread and transfer 4 cups to a large bowl. (Save any remaining crumbled cornbread for another use.) Add the crumbled biscuits to the cornbread, along with the onion and chicken broth. Melt the margarine in a small saucepan over medium heat and add to the cornbread mixture. Beat the eggs in a small bowl and add to the cornbread mixture, stirring until it takes on a batterlike consistency. Season with salt and pepper to taste. Transfer to the prepared baking dish and bake at 450°F for 40 minutes, or until a wooden skewer inserted into the center of the bread comes out clean. Let cool for several minutes before serving.

Loretta Lynn

FROM A DIRT-POOR EXISTENCE as a child in the hills of Kentucky, Loretta Lynn, with her songs about life and her heartfelt country vocals, has risen to heights rarely attained by an entertainer, man or woman. Since 1961, her songs—mostly from a woman's point of view— have dominated the charts with hit after hit.

Loretta's hardscrabble life story was told in the song "Coal Miner's Daughter," which became a number-one hit and spawned a successful book by the same title. A movie was made from the best-selling book, starring Sissy Spacek as Loretta. The movie was a giant success and remains a TV and DVD favorite.

THE FIRST CHRISTMAS after I started making some money was a mess. I love Christmas, but I just hated cleaning up the place. The kids got anything they wanted. There was nothing that they could eat that they didn't get, either. That was a bad thing, I think. I think it's nice to want just a little bit. When you get to where you don't want anymore, it's not good. When your kids come in and say, "I want a car for Christmas," you know it's bad.

The whole family still comes in every Thanksgiving and every Christmas. And I still cook for them. Everybody comes into the kitchen, but I shoo them into the front room. Sometimes, we'll do potluck. I cook the turkey and make the dressing. I put oysters in my dressing. The oysters make it more moist, but you can't taste them like you can by themselves. I cook the turkey and the dressing, green beans, and corn.

Potluck Christmas Dressing

I love making a big Christmas dinner for my family. The table is always full of my down-home country cooking, and one thing I always make is this dressing. The kids declared it a family tradition. Hope y'all like it. Serves 6

12 cups cubed day-old white bread or cornbread
4 cups chicken broth
$\frac{1}{2}$ pound (2 sticks) unsalted butter
2 large eggs
2 (8-ounce) cans sliced mushrooms, drained
1 pint fresh oysters, drained and chopped
1 cup chopped onions
1 cup diced celery
1 cup chopped pecans
$1\frac{1}{2}$ teaspoons salt
$1\frac{1}{2}$ teaspoons dried, crumbled sage
1 teaspoon poultry seasoning
1 teaspoon dried thyme
$\frac{1}{2}$ teaspoon cracked black pepper

1. Place the bread cubes and chicken broth in an electric slow cooker. Melt the butter in a small saucepan over medium heat and add to the bread mixture.

2. Beat the eggs in a small bowl and add to the cooker, along with the mushrooms, oysters, onions, celery, pecans, salt, sage, poultry seasoning, thyme, and pepper. Stir to blend, cover, and cook on high for 45 minutes. Turn the heat to low and cook for 4 hours more.

Candy Christmas

CANDY CHRISTMAS is a veteran performer with gospel roots that stretch back three generations. She is a descendant of members of the legendary Goodman's and Hemphill's gospel singing families. In 1973, at the age of thirteen, Candy recorded her first song, "I Came on Business for the King." It was a hit and climbed to number five on the gospel music charts. Candy has been featured on the Bill Gaither video project called *Gaither and Friends Revival.* She continues writing her own material, and has even written a book containing Cajun recipes from her years in Louisiana. The book contains wonderful anecdotes of her childhood and great pictures of her extended family.

Candy Christmas with her husband, Kent, and children, Josh, Jasmine, and Nicholas

MY DAD WAS THE SON of a minister, the tenth child in a family of fourteen. Every year, all his siblings would travel to my grandparents' house from all over the country with their growing families to share the holidays together. I'm not quite sure how we managed to crowd into my grandparents' tiny wood-framed house or around my grandmother's table, but I don't remember feeling crowded. I do remember the laughter and the love.

When Christmas dinner was finished and the dishes were washed and put away, our family would adjourn to the den where the Christmas tree and all its trimmings could barely be seen amid all the brightly wrapped packages that were haphazardly stacked nearly to the ceiling. The gifts were handed out one by one until nothing was left under the tree. Then my grandfather would signal us with a shout and the sound of paper tearing and shrieks of joy and excitement filled the room, as all the parcels were unwrapped at once.

At the end of the evening, we'd gather around my grandfather as he'd take out his well-worn Bible and begin to read. Every Christmas, he read about Mary and Joseph and how there was no room in the inn—about the shepherds keeping their sheep and the angels that sang glory to God in the highest and the wise men who brought their gifts of frankincense and myrrh. Each time I heard the story, it was as if it was the first time. It was new and fresh and alive in my mind's eye.

I am thankful for my sweet memories of Christmas and the holidays that I'll never forget, but most of all I am thankful for my rich heritage and being taught the true meaning of Christmas. It wasn't the turkey with all the trimmings or the gifts piled to the ceiling that made life rich, but it was our coming together as a family once a year to worship the Christ child who brought peace on earth and goodwill to men.

No-Turnin'-Back Corn Casserole

"Pass the dish one more time" is what you'll hear around your table when you serve this favorite. Make plenty to go around a second time. Serves 8 to 10

> 1 (7-ounce) package cornbread mix,
>   Mexican-style if possible
> 4 large eggs
> 3 (15-ounce) cans creamed corn
> 1½ cups grated very sharp Cheddar cheese
> 1 cup vegetable oil
> ¼ cup chopped pickled jalapeño peppers

1. Preheat the oven to 425°F. Grease a 13 by 9-inch baking dish.

2. Place the cornbread mix in a large bowl. Add the eggs, creamed corn, cheese, oil, and jalapeño peppers. Stir well to blend. Transfer to the prepared dish and bake for 20 minutes, or until a wooden skewer inserted into the center of the casserole comes out clean.

John Conlee

*J*OHN CONLEE looks at the world through rose-colored glasses, for a reason. In 1978, "Rose Colored Glasses," a song he had co-written with a newsman at his radio station, rocketed to the top of the country music charts. During the next decade, he scored hit after hit with songs from the heart and others that spoke to the working man.

MY FAVORITE CHRISTMAS was the year my sister, Helen, and I got cowgirl and cowboy regalia, a saddle for the horse, a bridle, boots, and cowboy hats. I was seven or eight that year and the incentive for me to get my first pony was to give up carrying my blanket. Of course, the pony was coming anyway.

I loved the smell of the Christmas tree we cut down on our farm. We decorated it with great big bows and rope, and traditional ornaments that weren't broken in the summertime when my sister and I played in the attic. And we hung the old-fashioned lights—when one went out you knew which one it was and you changed it. Not like the ones today, where if one goes out, they all do.

On Christmas Eve, my parents, my sister, my grandparents, and cousins got together for dinner. It was country ham and turkey and every other thing you could think of, including my favorite casserole—broccoli and cheese with crackers on top. I got the recipe from a lady who worked with me at the local funeral home, and I brought it home to Mom.

We had the big family Christmas Eve tradition well into my twenties. When we began to grow up and spread out, it became a smaller gathering. My sister, Helen, and I have a tradition of getting together in between Thanksgiving and Christmas to bake peanut brittle pie to share with our friends and family. Hope you and your loved ones enjoy your holiday moments as much as my family continues to do year after year.

Common Man's Broccoli and Cheese Casserole

This Kentucky farm boy brought this recipe home to Mom, who made it one of his favorite dishes on their holiday table. Serves 4

2 heads broccoli
1½ cups milk
4 tablespoons (½ stick) unsalted butter
½ cup chopped onion
3 tablespoons unbleached, all-purpose flour
1½ cups grated Cheddar cheese
Salt and cracked black pepper, to taste
1½ cups crushed Ritz crackers

1. Bring a large pot of water to a boil for cooking the broccoli. Cut the stalks from each head. Using a carrot peeler, peel off the tough outer skin of the stalks and cut them into ¼-inch-thick slices. Separate the florets.

2. Add the stalks to the boiling water and cook for 2 minutes. Add the florets and cook for 4 minutes. Drain and transfer to a large bowl to cool.

3. Preheat the oven to 350°F. Grease a 13 by 9-inch baking dish.

4. Place the milk in a small saucepan over medium heat. When almost boiling, turn off the heat and cover.

5. Melt the butter in a medium saucepan over medium-high heat. Add the onion and sauté until translucent, about 3 minutes. Stir in the flour and cook for 3 minutes. Remove the saucepan from the heat and whisk in the hot milk. Return the pan to the stove and continue whisking over medium heat until the sauce begins to bubble and thicken. Gradually add the cheese, about $1/4$ cup at a time, whisking constantly.

6. Pour the hot cheese sauce over the broccoli. Season with salt and pepper to taste and toss well to mix. Transfer to the prepared baking pan and evenly scatter with the crushed crackers. Bake for 20 minutes or until the casserole is hot and bubbling around the edges.

John Conlee with his sister, Helen

Brad Cotter

BRAD COTTER, the son of a preacher man, sang gospel music as a child, but spent eight long, discouraging years trying to find a way into the world of country music. Feeling that he had nothing to lose, he auditioned for USA Network's *Nashville Star* and to his surprise, he won. Epic Records signed him and he was immediately in demand. Now instead of pitching his songs to recording companies, aspiring songwriters are pitching to him. Brad is from Opelika, Alabama.

AS IS THE CASE with most kids, I must admit my favorite Christmas was the year I received my favorite gift. The year was 1979. I was nine years old and was already obsessed with cars and dreamed of one day racing them. I knew from being around several race shops and drivers that to be a good racer you had to have good feel for a car. The best way to learn that is to start out with something small that you can handle. I wanted a go-cart!

Dad and I finally convinced Mom to give us her blessing. But according to Dad, Santa didn't get the memo in time, so they would wait until after the holidays and I could get one then. I was sad and disappointed to say the least. Here we are just days away from the big day, and Dad breaks the news to me. Unknownst to him at the time, my aunts and cousins had already clued me in to the whole Santa Claus charade, so I was mad as I could be at Dad!

To make up for me not having anything from Santa that particular morning, my grandmother and Aunt Gladys suggested that my parents and I spend the night at my grandparents' house. This was out of the ordinary because my grandparents' farm was only twenty minutes from our house, and my grandmother already had a house full of relatives. So even though I was the only nine-year-old in the whole world who wasn't gonna get anything for Christmas, except socks and underwear, we'd all just enjoy each other's company, and maybe my cousin Gina would take turns with me on her go-cart. Somehow they convinced me this was okay.

I was awakened in the wee hours of the morning by a loud commotion and the belly laughs of my dad and granddaddy. You see, the Red Rally Sport 5-horsepower go-cart that had been hidden in the barn was a little difficult to get into the living room. Apparently my dad had dropped his end of it, and my granddaddy couldn't resist cracking up.

Needless to say, "Santa" came way early for everybody in the house that morning because I was so excited, I wouldn't let them go back to sleep. I can still remember that day after breakfast when they finally let me outside—I drove the wheels off that little go-cart. My cousin Gina brought hers to Grandmother's and my other cousin Tommy got one that year also. Somehow nobody got hurt that day at the "Ridge Grove Mini Speedway," but we all got a big kick out of the hurt little boy the night before who thought he was getting only underwear and socks for Christmas.

Patient Man's Squash Casserole

Grow it, gather up an armful, and bring it on in. (Or run on into town and buy a few.) We're cooking squash casserole. And this is one of the best squash recipes I've ever had. Truly worth waiting for. Serves 10 to 12

3 tablespoons vegetable oil

10 medium yellow summer squash, trimmed and thinly sliced

2 medium onions, chopped

12 tablespoons (1$^1/_2$ sticks) margarine or butter

2 large eggs

1$^1/_2$ teaspoons salt

$^1/_2$ teaspoon cracked black pepper

40 saltine crackers, crushed

1. Preheat the oven to 325°F. Coat a 3-quart casserole with nonstick cooking spray.

2. Place 1$^1/_2$ tablespoons of the oil in a large skillet over medium heat. When hot, add half of the squash and half of the onion. Sauté for 15 minutes. Transfer the vegetables to a large bowl and repeat the process with the remaining oil, squash, and onion. Using a potato masher, mash the squash and onion mixture.

3. Melt 8 tablespoons of the butter in a small saucepan and add it to the squash mixture. Add the eggs, salt, and pepper, and stir well to blend. Transfer the mixture to the prepared casserole.

4. Place the crushed saltines in a large bowl. Melt the remaining 4 tablespoons of butter in a small saucepan and pour over the crackers. Toss well to mix. Spread the buttered crackers evenly over the casserole and bake for 35 minutes, or until a knife or tester inserted in the middle comes out clean.

Brad Cotter (right) with his friends

Bobby Goldsboro

BOBBY GOLDSBORO began his professional career in the early 1960s as a guitarist with the legendary Roy Orbison. In 1964 he had his first hit single with "See the Funny Little Clown." That year he opened for the Rolling Stones for their first U.S. tour. More hits followed, including his 1968 classic "Honey," which brought him international prominence. "Watching Scotty Grow," "Little Green Apples," and "With Pen in Hand" were more Goldsboro classics. These songs, along with his comedic talent, have made Bobby a national television favorite and a household name.

Bobby and Diane Goldsboro

I GREW UP in Marianna, Florida. We lived on a hill on a busy highway. By the time I was ten years old I had stopped asking for a bicycle for Christmas. "Too dangerous," said my father. So when Christmas morning came my father asked me, "If you could have anything in the world, what would it be?" Without hesitation I screamed, "A contract to play second base for the Cleveland Indians!" It hadn't dawned on me that there weren't too many ten-year-olds playing in the Major Leagues. The look on my father's face told me immediately that a Major League contract wasn't my Christmas present. So I then blurted out, "A swimming pool!" With a look of disgust my father walked out of the room. Then I heard a bell ringing in the next room. "An electric train!" When I ran into the room I saw a Schwinn bicycle. My father must have thought, "Well, maybe a bicycle was his fourth choice!" I had put a bicycle completely out of my mind. I must have stood there for several seconds, thinking I must be dreaming.

Over the next few days I hardly let the bicycle out of my sight. I was told not to ride in the street. Naturally, I came home one day and decided to coast down the hill. When I saw a mail truck in front of our house, I panicked. I completely forgot how to put on the brakes and slammed right into the back of that truck. I stopped but the bike kept going, right underneath the truck. I jumped up and looked for the bike. It was in front of the truck and there wasn't a scratch on it. In a flash I had the bike in my yard, pushing it into the garage. I never told my father, but you can believe I had learned my lesson.

It's funny, the things you remember from your childhood. I can't recall ever having a bad Christmas, and I'm sure I got pretty much everything I ever wanted. I never did play for the Cleveland Indians. I did get an electric train, and I eventually got a swimming pool—after I grew up. But the bicycle will always be the best memory.

Little Things
Garlic Mashed Potatoes and Green Beans with Tomatoes

The hectic life my wife, Diane, and I live, with our many projects and travels, doesn't always allow time to plan ahead and prepare for a flavorful menu at mealtime. These recipes are not only easy but add a little something special to any meal. During the holidays we are all busy shopping, wrapping, decorating, and visiting friends and family, with little time to spare. If you prepare one of these favorites, how quick and simple they are can be your secret. Serves 4

Garlic Mashed Potatoes

1 (20-ounce) package prepared mashed potatoes (available in the supermarket refrigerator section)
1 cup shredded Cheddar cheese
1/2 teaspoon garlic salt
1/4 teaspoon liquid smoke

Combine the potatoes, cheese, garlic salt, and liquid smoke in a medium-size microwave-safe bowl. Stir well to blend. Cover the bowl and microwave the potatoes on high for 3 minutes. Remove the potatoes and stir well. Cover and microwave for 3 more minutes or until the potatoes are hot through.

Green Beans with Tomatoes

2 (14 1/2-ounce) cans green beans, drained
1 (14 1/2-ounce) can stewed tomatoes
Salt and cracked black pepper, to taste

Combine the green beans and stewed tomatoes in a medium saucepan over medium heat. Bring to a boil, reduce the heat to low, and simmer for 10 minutes. Season with salt and pepper to taste.

Margo Smith

ARGO SMITH's original song, "There, I Said It," was released in 1975. She followed her hit debut record with numerous other top-ten hits. Three of them, "Little Things Mean a Lot," "Don't Break the Hearts That Love You," and "It Only Hurts for a Little While," reached the number one position. In 1978, with singer Rex Allen Jr., she recorded "Cup of Tea," which won them a nomination for the top duet of the year from both the Academy of Country Music and Music City News. Margo and her daughter, Holly, have had several number one Christian country records, and in 1993 and 1994 were elected top duet of the year by the International Country Gospel Association. Her many talents include a world-class yodeling ability.

Margo Smith (top row) with her family

I WAS BORN in Ohio, part of a big family. We had awesome Christmases. My momma taught us all how to cook, even the boys. When we all got together, the main thing was food. We didn't have a lot of money, so everyone received one gift maybe and that was it. We loved all the old Christmas songs, which we sang around the piano.

I remember my favorite Christmas well. It was the year I had turned seventeen years old and I was about to graduate from high school. I was on the student council, and members of the council were all supposed to provide a Christmas gift for a needy child. During those times money was scarce in my family, but I was committed and I really wanted to give something special. I tried to come up with something that would equal what I knew the other kids would be doing but to no avail.

As I sat in my room pondering what to do, I glanced over at my big beautiful teddy bear. I had just received the bear from my boyfriend, who had won it for me at the fair. I loved that bear and I loved the boy who gave it to me. As difficult as it was, I just couldn't think of anything else that I could give that would measure up, so I made the decision to give away the bear.

With tears in my eyes I went to the home of the little boy who was to receive my present. He was blind and that bear made his Christmas. You can imagine it made mine, too.

Take-My-Breath-Away Vegetable Casserole

I've found the secret to getting the kids to eat their veggies. I just cover them with lots and lots of melted cheese in this casserole. They love it! We already have our Christmas party on the calendar. And you can be sure this casserole will be there. Serves 6

1 (10-ounce) package frozen broccoli florets, thawed

1 (10-ounce) package frozen cauliflower florets, thawed

1 (10-ounce) package frozen Brussels sprouts, thawed

1 (10-ounce) package frozen sliced carrots, thawed

1 (10½-ounce) can cream of celery soup

1 (4-ounce) jar Cheez Whiz

1 (10½-ounce) can fried onion rings

1. Preheat the oven to 375°F. Grease a 13 by 9-inch baking dish.

2. Drain the vegetables and place in a large bowl. Add the soup and Cheez Whiz and stir to blend. Transfer to the prepared baking dish and bake for 30 minutes.

3. Scatter the onion rings evenly over the casserole and bake for 5 minutes more.

Jeff Cook

$\mathcal{S}$INCE THE AGE OF THIRTEEN, Jeff Cook has been playing lead guitar and keyboard in local bands. One of the founding fathers of the group Alabama, Jeff and his bandmates have been named Entertainers of the Year eight times. They have a string of forty number-one singles spanning two decades and have become one of the top-selling groups of all times. Alabama was inducted into the Country Music Hall of Fame in 2005.

Jeff Cook and his wife, Lisa, with their dog, Barkley

KARAOKE IS KING at my house on Christmas. It has become our favorite form of entertainment. Each family member gets up and sings—good or bad—with a musical track of his or her choice. My favorite Christmas song is always "Silent Night." Every year after dinner, we repeat this tradition and everyone looks forward to it.

We decorate three trees with old and new decorations. The biggest tree, twenty feet tall, is placed in our family room, where we all gather to enjoy sharing our gifts. The other two trees along with many other beautiful decorations are spread about our home, which is built like a castle.

Pa Rumpa Pom Pom Rum Muffins

My contribution to the Christmas feast is a favorite of all who sit down to eat. Enjoy the flavor of these soft, moist rum muffins.
Makes 24 muffins

Muffins

1 (18.25-ounce) package yellow cake mix

1 (3.4-ounce) box instant banana cream pudding and pie filling mix

4 large eggs

1/2 cup dark rum

1/2 cup vegetable oil

1 cup chopped walnuts

Glaze

8 tablespoons (1 stick) unsalted butter

1 cup sugar

1/2 cup dark rum

1. To make the muffins: Preheat the oven to 325°F. Coat two 12-cup muffin tins with nonstick cooking spray.

2. Combine the cake and pudding mixes in a large bowl. Add the eggs, 1/2 cup of water, the rum, and oil and stir to mix. Blend in the walnuts. Divide the batter between the muffin tins, filling cups 2/3 full, and bake for 25 minutes, or until a wooden skewer inserted in the center of one muffin comes out clean. Let the muffins cool for 5 minutes in their tins before transferring to wire racks to cool.

3. To make the glaze: Melt the butter in a small saucepan over medium heat. Add the sugar and 1/4 cup of water and bring to a boil. Boil over medium heat for 5 minutes, stirring constantly. Turn off the heat and stir in the rum.

4. Arrange the muffins on a decorative serving plate. Using a toothpick, prick the top of each muffin in several places and drizzle with the glaze. Continue drizzling the muffins with the glaze until it is used up.

Vince Gill

*I*T TAKES ONLY A FEW WORDS to explain why Vince Gill is so important in the world of country music: fifteen Grammys and eighteen Country Music Association awards—including Entertainer of the Year twice and Song of the Year four times. In fact, Vince is the biggest CMA winner in history. A member of the *Grand Ole Opry,* he has sold twenty-two million records, making him one of country music's top sellers. In March 2000, Vince married Amy Grant, one of contemporary Christian music's biggest stars. Amy has also enjoyed great success as a crossover artist in the pop music genre. Vince and Amy have a daughter, Corrina, and they live in Nashville, Tennessee.

Vince Gill and his sister, Gina

MANY HALL OF FAME members have touched listeners' hearts with holiday songs. There's Brenda Lee, of course, with her perennial classic "Rockin' Around the Christmas Tree." Then there's Bill Monroe, whose rendition of "Christmas Time's a-Comin'" is still a favorite with bluegrass fans around the world. And of course, who could forget "Blue Christmas," recorded by Elvis Presley? But I'll bet most folks don't know that Ernest Tubb, the Texas Troubadour, had a number one hit with this song in 1949—years before Elvis made his first recording. There's Tex Ritter's "Christmas Carols by the Old Corral" (number two in 1945), Eddy Arnold's "Christmas Can't Be Far Away," and "Christmas in Dixie," a hit for Alabama, one of the Hall of Fame's most recent inductees.

May there be peace on earth every Christmas. When you visit us during the Christmas holidays at the Country Music Hall of Fame, I know you'll enjoy one of my favorite happenings: when the stars drop by to sing and share their Christmas thoughts around the Christmas tree just for you!

Turn Me Loose Grandmother Lucy's Homemade Rolls

Personally, the holidays for me bring back memories of my family gatherings with all the traditional trimmings at Grandmother Lucy's home. We savored her homemade rolls the most. We never knew her special ingredients at the time, but we did know that she sure added a right smart bit of love. Makes 12 rolls

2 cups milk

1 (1/4-ounce) package dry yeast

1/4 cup sugar

1 large egg

1/4 cup unsalted butter, melted, plus more for brushing the rolls, if desired

2 teaspoons salt

2 cups unbleached, all-purpose flour, plus more for dusting

1. Place the milk in a medium saucepan over medium-high heat. When almost boiling, pour it into a large bowl. Let the milk cool to 110°F.

2. Add the yeast and sugar to the milk and stir to blend; let the mixture stand for 5 minutes to dissolve the yeast.

3. Whisk in the egg, followed by 1/4 cup of the melted butter and the salt. Stir in the flour until the mixture forms a soft dough.

4. Lightly dust a clean work surface with flour. Transfer the dough to the floured surface and knead for several minutes by hand until the dough becomes smooth and elastic. Grease a large bowl, shape the dough into a ball, and cover the bowl with plastic wrap. Let the dough rise in a warm place until nearly doubled in bulk, 1 to 1 1/2 hours.

5. Punch down the dough to deflate and shape it into a ball. Return the dough to the greased bowl and seal with plastic wrap. Let the dough rise again, this time for 20 minutes.

6. Preheat the oven to 350°F. Grease a 12-cup muffin tin.

7. Punch down the dough for a second time and turn it out onto a clean work surface lightly dusted with flour. Roll the dough to a 1/2-inch thickness. Using a 2-inch cookie cutter or other utensil, cut out 36 circles of dough, rerolling the scraps as necessary, and roll each circle into a ball. Place three balls in each muffin cup so that they form a cloverleaf pattern. If you want glossy rolls, brush the tops of the balls with melted butter. Bake the rolls for 15 to 20 minutes or until they appear light brown and make a hollow sound when the bottoms are tapped. Remove the rolls from the muffin tin and let cool on a wire rack.

Sara Evans

RAISED ON A FARM in Missouri, Sara Evans started singing every weekend in her family's band at the age of five. Moving permanently to Nashville in 1995, Sara was discovered by Country Music Hall of Fame songwriter Harlan Howard who urged RCA to give her a listen. Although Harlan is no longer with us, Sara is everything that he thought she could be and more. Her first outings met with some resistance from country radio because of her back-to-basics country sound; but then in 1998 "No Place That Far" became her first number one record, followed by "Born to Fly." And fly she did.

CHRISTMAS MORNING in our family is all about tradition. As well as the excitement about the gifts under our tree, everyone looks forward to our Christmas breakfast, especially the homemade cinnamon rolls. The cinnamon rolls are a recipe that goes back to my grandmother and was passed down to my mother and me. With seven children and twelve grandchildren, there never seem to be enough to satisfy everyone's appetite for the cinnamon rolls.

Of course, there is more to the breakfast. We also have biscuits with sausage gravy, scrambled eggs, country ham, fried potatoes, fresh squeezed orange juice, chocolate milk, and coffee.

Leaving the breakfast mess in the kitchen, everyone rushes to the TV room to a tree surrounded by piles of gifts. After the gifts are passed out and opened, the event is usually followed by a paper-throwing battle using paper balls made from the torn wrapping paper. One thing is guaranteed: Paper balls will be found behind furniture and other remote places for days to come.

We all love getting together on Christmas morning, and this traditional breakfast gives everyone a chance to spend time with family we don't get to see very often. We look forward to continuing this tradition for many years to come.

Born to Fly Cinnamon Rolls

Everyone looks forward to our traditional Christmas breakfast, and these homemade cinnamon rolls are a special treat. Makes 2 dozen

Rolls

1 cup milk

$\frac{1}{2}$ cup granulated sugar

$\frac{1}{2}$ teaspoon salt

5 cups unbleached, all-purpose flour, plus more for dusting

2 large eggs

1 ($\frac{1}{4}$-ounce) package dry yeast

1 cup firmly packed light brown sugar

3 tablespoons cinnamon

5 tablespoons unsalted butter

Glaze

1 cup confectioner's sugar

1. To make the rolls: Heat the milk in a medium saucepan over medium-high heat. When almost boiling, turn off the heat. Add the granulated sugar and salt and stir until dissolved.

2. Transfer the milk mixture to a large bowl. Add 2 cups of the flour and stir until mixed. Blend in the eggs.

3. Place the yeast in a small bowl and blend with $\frac{1}{2}$ cup warm water. When the yeast has dissolved, add to the flour mixture and stir to blend. Add the remaining 3 cups of flour and stir well to form a soft dough.

4. Lightly dust a clean work surface with flour. Transfer the dough to the floured surface and knead for several minutes by hand until the dough becomes smooth and elastic. Grease a large bowl, shape the dough into a ball, and cover the bowl with plastic wrap. Let the dough rise in a warm place until nearly doubled in bulk, 1 to $1\frac{1}{2}$ hours.

5. Meanwhile, whisk together the brown sugar and cinnamon in a small bowl. Set aside. Grease a large baking sheet.

6. Just before the dough has finished rising, melt the butter in a small saucepan over medium heat. Set aside to cool slightly.

7. Punch down the dough to deflate. Lightly dust a clean work surface with flour and roll out the dough so that it forms a $\frac{1}{2}$-inch-thick rectangle. Brush the melted butter over the dough. Then sprinkle the cinnamon-sugar mixture over the top. Roll up the dough, as if forming a jellyroll, until you have a large cylinder. Using a sharp knife, cut the cylinder into 1-inch-thick slices and place on the prepared baking sheet. Cover the rolls with a damp cloth and let rise for 20 minutes.

8. Preheat the oven to 375°F.

9. Bake the rolls for 15 to 20 minutes or until puffed and golden. Let cool slightly.

10. To make the glaze: Place the confectioner's sugar in a bowl. Add 2 tablespoons of hot water and stir to create a smooth, spreadable icing. Using a knife or pastry tube, spread or squeeze some icing onto each roll.

Sara Evans and her husband, Craig Schelske

Bill Anderson

AT THE AGE OF NINETEEN, Bill Anderson, one of America's greatest musical poets, broke onto the country music scene with his song "City Lights." He has been one of the most enduring country music entertainers in the industry, selling millions of records, and has certainly been one of the most honored songwriters. He has been a television game show host, soap opera star, spokesman for a nationwide restaurant chain, and author of two books; Bill is now a satellite radio country music host. His extensive stream of hits is unsurpassed; and even today, almost five decades after his start, he continues to write hit after hit for the biggest names in country music. He has definitely earned his recent membership in the Country Music Hall of Fame.

I MUST HAVE BEEN about ten years old the Christmas I nearly drove my parents crazy asking for a bicycle. When they had inquired as to what I might like under the tree on Christmas morning I confessed to having a one-track, two-wheeled mind. I wanted that shiny blue Columbia brand bicycle I had seen in the window at Jenkins Cycle Shop. I wanted nothing more, but I wasn't going to be happy with anything less. But I knew that money was tight, the future was uncertain, and bicycles didn't come cheap.

Waiting made me a nervous disaster, and I nursed a queasy, taunting feeling deep in the pit of my stomach that seemed to whisper, "It ain't gonna happen boy, it ain't gonna happen." By three o'clock Christmas Eve afternoon I was exhausted. I flipped on my tableside radio to find some live country music; but instead, I heard the anxious voice of our local announcer: "Firemen have just been called to Jenkins Cycle Shop on Church Street where a giant blaze is threatening to destroy the building." My heart sank.

My imagination immediately got busy painting all sorts of depressing pictures. I could just see my beautiful blue bicycle reduced to a pile of charred, smoking rubbish. It was about to be the most depressing Christmas anyone had ever been forced to endure.

I waited for what seemed an eternity. Then, a few minutes past eight o'clock, I finally looked out my bedroom window and saw the headlights from my parents' car. Dad opened the door on the driver's side and got out. When he did, the dome light inside the car came on and I saw it! Before Dad could close the doors and come inside, I feasted my eyes on the body of the most gorgeous, shiny blue bicycle that ever existed in the whole wide world. I raised my arms in triumph. My bike had survived the fire. I was going to get my Christmas wish after all.

The next morning I tried real hard to act surprised. Dad said solemnly, "They had a real bad fire at Jenkins yesterday afternoon. There were over fifty bicycles in the store at the time. Yours must have been parked close to the door. It was one of only eight they were able to save." I was thrilled, but I wasn't so excited that I didn't hurt for the other forty-plus kids who had been wanting and expecting bicycles for Christmas and who, I knew, were now terribly disappointed.

I hugged my mom and dad, hopped on the bike, and roared off down the sidewalk. I knew boys my age weren't supposed to believe in Santa Claus, but I wasn't so sure. Santa Claus, or somebody an awful lot like him, had sure been mighty good to me!

Whispering Mistletoe Cranberry Bread

The memories of smelling my grandmother's cranberry bread and having a big glass of milk still bring a smile to my face! Makes 1 large loaf

2 cups unbleached, all-purpose flour

1 cup sugar

1½ teaspoons baking powder

1 teaspoon salt

½ teaspoon baking soda

4 tablespoons (½ stick) unsalted butter or margarine

1 large egg

1 teaspoon grated orange zest

¾ cup fresh orange juice

1½ cups golden raisins

1½ cups fresh or frozen chopped cranberries

1. Preheat the oven to 350°F. Grease one 9-inch loaf pan.

2. Whisk together the flour, sugar, baking powder, salt, and baking soda in a large bowl. With a pastry blender or fork, cut in the butter until the mixture is crumbly. Add the egg, orange zest, and orange juice and stir to blend. Mix in the raisins and cranberries.

3. Spoon the batter into the prepared pan and bake for 55 to 60 minutes, or until a wooden skewer inserted into the center of the loaf comes out clean. Let the bread cool in the pan for 10 minutes before inverting onto a wire rack to cool completely.

Crystal Gayle

CRYSTAL GAYLE can be described as a classic. Her beautiful voice and singing style transcend the boundaries of time and musical genres. Always in vogue, her songs touch the heart of country and pop audiences everywhere. Crystal's signature song, "Don't It Make My Brown Eyes Blue," and her radiant beauty, enhanced by her ankle-length hair, make her recognizable around the world. Her lists of platinum and gold records and awards are extraordinary. Crystal and her husband, Bill, reside in Nashville, Tennessee.

Crystal Gayle with her children, Chris and Catherine

I AM THE YOUNGEST of eight children, and when I was growing up my older brothers and sisters had already left home to start families of their own. My favorite Christmas memories are of everyone coming back home to visit. I love our whole family being together for Christmas.

When Bill Gatzimos and I were first married and he was still in college, we went out to the woods and cut down a Christmas tree. We dragged it about a half mile to the car and carried it to our apartment. It hadn't looked so big out in the open, but in the apartment it was so wide that it took over half of the room. We decorated the tree with strings of popcorn and cranberries and other decorations that we made.

One morning we got up and there was a little mouse standing on his tippy toes on top of one of the packages, just high enough to reach and nibble on the decorations. We just stood and watched him for a while as he made himself a part of our Christmas memories.

Now on Christmas Eve we have a tradition. With our family we have a picnic of cheese, fruit, paté, Ritz crackers, and wine. On Christmas Day, lots of the family members come over. There are many good cooks in our family, and we cook a big meal and feast together that afternoon. Our Christmas tree is covered with ornaments. When the children, Catherine and Chris, were small, one of my fans crocheted little mailboxes with each of our family's names on them. They are small, but you can open them and tuck in little notes.

I have been traveling and performing Christmas concerts for several years, and our family's retail store is so busy during the holidays that we don't have time to do a lot of things in the community. I make sure to be home in plenty of time, though, so I can start baking about four days before Christmas. We have so many wonderful Christmas memories; each year is special in its own way. Hope your holidays are special, too.

Pumpkin Tea Bread to Make Your Brown Eyes Blue

When Bill and I were first married, I began baking this delicious pumpkin tea bread. Over the years, the recipe has been improved by adding nuts. It is a family tradition and a must for our Christmas breakfast. Makes 2 large loaves

$2^2/_3$ cups sugar
$2/_3$ cup vegetable oil or butter
4 large eggs
1 (16-ounce) can unsweetened pumpkin purée
$3^1/_3$ cups unbleached, all-purpose flour
2 teaspoons baking soda
$1^1/_2$ teaspoons salt
1 teaspoon ground cinnamon
1 teaspoon ground cloves
$1/_2$ teaspoon baking powder
$2/_3$ cup chopped nuts, such as walnuts, optional

1. Preheat the oven to 350°F. Grease two 9-inch loaf pans.

2. Combine the sugar and oil in a large bowl and beat until well blended. Beat in the eggs, one at a time, followed by the pumpkin purée and $2/_3$ cup water.

3. Whisk together the flour, baking soda, salt, cinnamon, cloves, and baking powder in a medium bowl. Add to the pumpkin mixture and stir until just blended. Stir in the nuts, if using. Divide the batter between the prepared loaf pans and bake for 50 to 55 minutes, or until a wooden skewer inserted into the center of one loaf comes out clean. Let each loaf cool in its pan for 10 minutes before inverting onto a wire rack to cool completely.

Jim Nabors

WHEREVER HE GOES, people old and young run up to Jim Nabors, crying, "Say it, say it"; and Jim, smiling at each and every one, responds with his signature "Golleee." The fans giggle with glee, happy that they have heard the famous and funny singer-actor fill their request. Jim has legions of friends from every walk of life, each one claiming to be his best. His easygoing demeanor and Southern gentleman friendliness make everyone comfortable to be in his presence. So, it's no wonder that Jim has touched the world with his comedic skills, making him one of the most well known entertainers the world over.

Jim Nabors with his godchild, Madeline Hahnsfield

CHRISTMAS IN HAWAII always reminds me of how fortunate I am to have had a second home and macadamia nut farm in Hana on the island of Maui for the last twenty years. I have many varieties of bananas and other fruits as well as tropical flowers on my property. The soil is so rich that I often have an overabundance of bananas. Since I can't eat or give them away fast enough, I've learned to bake a great banana bread with macadamia nuts.

The joy of preparing this recipe is a double treat during Christmas, because I serve this special bread to guests and sometimes send them home with an extra loaf. I grew up in Alabama and have wonderful memories of Christmas in the South, too. On Christmas Day, I enjoy watching my godchild and her parents open up their surprises. The best holiday gifts are those you can give.

Maui Banana Bread

I hope you will enjoy this recipe, and if you make it at Christmas, I hope you will be reminded of Hawaii and the aloha that is unique to the Hawaiian culture. I think of aloha as the spirit of Christmas all year long. Happy holiday baking!

Makes 2 large loaves

$1/2$ pound (2 sticks) unsalted butter, softened, or 1 cup vegetable oil
2 cups sugar
4 large eggs
6 medium very ripe bananas, peeled and mashed
$2^1/2$ cups unbleached, all-purpose flour
2 teaspoons baking soda
1 teaspoon salt
$1/2$ cup chopped macadamia nuts

1. Preheat the oven to 350°F. Grease two 9-inch loaf pans.

2. Combine the butter with the sugar in a large bowl. Using electric beaters, beat the mixture until creamy and pale yellow. Beat in the eggs, one at a time, then add the bananas.

3. Sift together the flour, baking soda, and salt into a medium bowl. Add to the banana mixture and stir until incorporated. Mix in the nuts. Divide the batter between the two prepared pans and bake for 50 to 60 minutes, or until a wooden skewer inserted into the center of one loaf comes out clean. Let each loaf cool in its pan for 10 minutes before inverting onto a wire rack to cool completely.

Willie Nelson

WILLIE NELSON is an American musical icon. A poet in his own right, he has transcended countless musical genres. From country and blues to pop and reggae, Willie's unique style has continued to attract fans of all ages worldwide. His commitment to humanity can be heard in his powerful lyrics and felt through his support of countless organizations, including Farm Aid, an organization he started to support the independent farmer. Willie's special ability to relate to his audience has taken him from the big stage to the big screen; he has appeared in countless films and television programs. In addition, he has written and been the focus of numerous books over the past four decades. He, along with his band—which features his sister, Bobbie, on piano—continues to tour the world. A living legend, Willie is truly one of the finest singers and songwriters of our time.

Told by Bobbie Nelson (Willie's sister)

CHRISTMAS WAS a lot different for us growing up than it is today. We never had a Christmas tree and couldn't afford presents. Instead, we decorated my grandma's biggest potted oleander bush and called it our Christmas tree. We decorated it with whatever we could find, like popcorn balls and a garland made from red and green construction paper links we made at school.

Sometimes people would bring us gifts. I remember one year someone gave me some little dishes, along with a small stove and refrigerator. They weren't new, but it didn't matter. Willie would use the stove to make our mud pies. The sun would bake them and we would eat them! I preferred the real food we got at Christmastime. Willie was a great playmate. He was very patient and would even play along with me and the paper dolls I made from the old Sears catalogs. But he could only take that so long. Eventually, we would put the dolls in Willie's truck.

Willie Nelson with his sister, Bobbie

In particular, I remember my grandma's buttermilk biscuits and chocolate gravy with hot chocolate. The chocolate looked like gravy but tasted like chocolate pudding. Grandma made hot chocolate like nobody else because it was all the old-fashioned way; she used Hershey's cocoa powder. It was delicious! Christmas was simple for Will and me, but it was as rich as our shared chocolate recipes.

Always on My Mind Biscuits and Chocolate Gravy with Cocoa

Grandma made our Christmases simply chocolaty with her buttermilk biscuits and chocolate gravy. We count Grandma's chocolate recipes among our Christmas treasures, and we think of her often.
Serves 12

Biscuits

2¹/₂ cups self-rising white flour
1¹/₂ teaspoons baking powder
¹/₂ teaspoon sugar
¹/₄ teaspoon baking soda
4 tablespoons (¹/₂ stick) unsalted butter
1 cup buttermilk
Flour for dusting

Chocolate Gravy

1¹/₂ cups sugar
2 tablespoons unsweetened cocoa powder
1 tablespoon unbleached, all-purpose flour
1 teaspoon vanilla extract
2 tablespoons cornstarch, optional

Cocoa

1¹/₄ cups sugar
²/₃ cup unsweetened cocoa powder
3 quarts milk

1. To make the biscuits: Preheat the oven to 450°F. Grease a baking sheet.

2. Whisk together the flour, baking powder, sugar, and baking soda in a large bowl. With a pastry blender or fork, cut in the butter until the mixture is crumbly. Stir in the buttermilk and mix until a soft dough forms. Turn the dough out onto a clean work surface dusted with flour and pat into a 3/4-inch-thick circle. Using a 2-inch round cutter or glass, cut the dough into 12 biscuits, gently reshaping the scraps as necessary. Place the biscuits on the prepared baking sheet and bake for approximately 8 minutes or until puffed and golden brown. Transfer to a wire rack to cool slightly.

3. To make the chocolate gravy: Whisk together the sugar, cocoa powder, and flour in a medium saucepan. Slowly whisk in 3 cups of water, followed by the vanilla. Turn the heat to medium and bring the mixture to a boil. Reduce the heat to low and simmer for 10 minutes, whisking constantly. To create a thicker gravy, blend together the cornstarch with 2 tablespoons of cold water in a small bowl. Transfer this mix to the chocolate gravy and whisk the gravy over low heat until thickened.

4. To make the cocoa: Whisk together the sugar and cocoa powder in a soup pot. Whisk in 4 cups of water, followed by the milk. Turn the heat to medium and bring the mixture to a boil, whisking often. Turn off the heat.

5. To serve, cut each warm biscuit in half horizontally. Lay both halves, cut side up, in a bowl. Spoon the warm chocolate gravy over the biscuits and serve with a mug of hot cocoa.

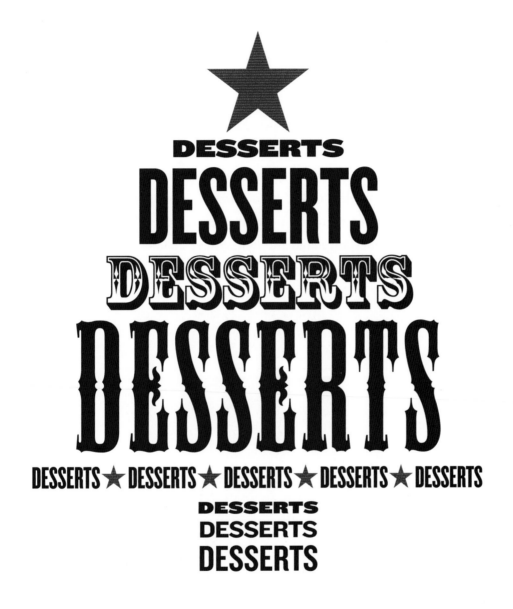

DESSERTS

DESSERTS

DESSERTS

DESSERTS

DESSERTS ★ DESSERTS ★ DESSERTS ★ DESSERTS ★ DESSERTS

DESSERTS

DESSERTS

DESSERTS

Keith Anderson

KEITH ANDERSON'S first days in Nashville were not auspicious. He arrived in Music City in the spring of 1998 in a broken-down car with two thousand dollars he had managed to save. To support himself he went to work as a waiter at a restaurant on Music Row. He says he was a terrible waiter, but he met a lot of music industry folks. He began working with some of country music's best writers and he made the rounds at songwriter shows in local nightclubs. Then in 2000 he put his own band together, and in 2002 the group won the Jim Beam Country Band Search. Within months he was drawing standing-room-only crowds, which led to an Arista Records contract. His debut single, "Pickin' Wildflowers," established him as a recording artist and his songs, which have been recorded by such artists as Garth Brooks, George Jones, and Gretchen Wilson, leave no question about his songwriting abilities. Keith Anderson has superstardom written all over him.

Keith Anderson with his brothers, Brian and Jason

CHRISTMAS WAS AMAZING when I was growing up. My mom was famous for her holiday baking, and she would start baking cookies in November. Our freezer was full of cookies: ginger snaps with a Hershey's kiss in the middle, butterscotch, and my favorite—chocolate cookies with peanut butter chips. You name it, Mom would fix it for the holidays, including peanut brittle, pecan pie, and pumpkin pie.

But my most favorite Christmas was just a few years ago. For about six years in a row, I wasn't making much money and couldn't even get home more than maybe twice a year. In fact, I could barely live on what I was making with the band, so I had no money to buy gifts at all. My gift was coming home to see everybody.

That Christmas, I was working for the wife of one of the guys who would later become part of my band. I was a cologne model at a store doing what we called "squirt and flirt." In other words I sprayed cologne on a card, handed it to the lady shoppers, and tried to get them to buy the cologne. I was getting ready to go back home for Christmas when the woman I was working for gathered up a bunch of samples and put together gift baskets for everyone in my family.

My car was in bad shape but I loaded it up with the baskets of perfume, lotion, and aftershave. I was so excited as I drove home to Oklahoma to give everyone their gifts. They were just happy to have me home.

Now that I have been busy on the road, it will be good to return home for the holidays not only to visit everyone but to get a little rest. It is great to be able to give gifts to those you care about, but really spending time together and enjoying this special time of year with them is the most important thing. There is simply nothing like the feeling I have with my family at Christmastime.

XXL Peanut Butter Balls

Coming home for the holidays is great. And one of the foods I want to find there are these peanut butter balls. You're sure to score lots of points with the family when you make them for the holidays. I can't wait to bite into this delicious dessert. Makes 20 balls

2 cups confectioner's sugar
1½ cups creamy peanut butter
4 tablespoons (½ stick) unsalted butter
1 (12-ounce) package semisweet chocolate chips
1 ounce (¼ bar) paraffin wax, finely chopped
1 box of toothpicks

1. Combine the sugar, peanut butter, and butter in a large bowl. Stir well to blend. Using your hands, pinch off a piece of the peanut butter mixture and roll it into a ball about the size of a walnut. Continue making the balls in this manner with the remaining mixture; you should have 20 balls. Place the balls on a baking sheet and refrigerate for 2 hours.

2. Grease a baking sheet.

3. Melt the chocolate chips and paraffin in the top of a double boiler. Stir until the mixture is blended and completely smooth.

4. Using a toothpick, pierce a peanut butter ball and dip it into the melted chocolate, twirling it slightly to coat. Place it on the prepared baking sheet. Continue dipping the remaining peanut butter balls in this same manner. Chill the balls in the refrigerator for several hours to set the chocolate.

Steve Azar

WHEN STEVE AZAR was four, he banged around on a toy guitar. By the time he was ten, he had put away the toy and gone for the real thing. That was the beginning. By the time he was fourteen years old, he had written four songs that he felt were good enough to take to Nashville. The seeds were sown. During college, the Steve Azar Band played throughout the Southeast, gaining legions of fans. Steve moved to Nashville in 1991 from his home in Greenville, Mississippi. By the end of his second day in Music City, he had been offered three exclusive songwriting contracts. In 2001, Steve had his first hit record with "I Don't Have to Be Me ('Til Monday)" and, in 2002, a number one video hit with "Waiting on Joe." His extraordinary songwriting gift and unique vocal delivery portend a great future for the Mercury recording artist.

CHRISTMAS IS ALWAYS a time of year to celebrate life! I have always been taught to appreciate the value of Christmas, why we celebrate it, and what it means. But my clearest memory, and one that obviously has impacted my life since, was the Christmas I asked for a real guitar.

I was twelve years old and was able to get around on the old guitar I had just well enough to want to upgrade. My folks both worked hard, although I was really not old enough to appreciate how difficult it would be for them to buy me a new guitar. But somehow they made it happen; what a wonderful gift. All I can say now is that they must have really worked Santa over that particular Christmas!

Now that I am a parent, I see Christmastime in a whole new light. Being able to start my own family traditions, watching my kids light up on Christmas morning, and helping them understand and appreciate the true meaning of this sacred holiday are the things that for me make this the most cherished season of the year.

Old Muddy Mississippi Mud Pie

As a kid, raised in the Mississippi Delta, I wasn't on the receiving end of many white Christmases. But one thing we did have going for us was pie. The pie that is most memorable to me is the Mississippi mud pie either my mom or my grandmother would make every year. They made it in a baking dish instead of in a pie plate so that they could feed the whole family: I wasn't the only one in the family who considered this an irresistible delicacy! It was hands-down my favorite part of the whole meal. **Serves 15**

Crust

1¼ cups graham cracker crumbs
⅓ cup sugar
⅓ cup unsalted butter

Filling

2 cups sugar
½ pound (2 sticks) unsalted butter, softened

4 large eggs

1 teaspoon vanilla extract

1½ cups unbleached, all-purpose flour

½ cup unsweetened cocoa powder

1 (13-ounce) jar marshmallow cream

Topping

1 (1-pound) box confectioner's sugar

½ cup unsweetened cocoa powder

8 tablespoons (1 stick) unsalted butter, softened

6 tablespoons milk

1 teaspoon vanilla extract

½ cup chopped pecan pieces, optional

1. Preheat the oven to 350°F.

2. To make the crust: Place the graham cracker crumbs and sugar in a medium bowl. Melt the butter in a small saucepan over medium heat. Add to the crumb mixture and stir well to mix. Transfer to a 13 by 9-inch baking dish and with your hands or the back of a wooden spoon press the crumbs in an even layer across the bottom of the dish. Bake for 5 to 7 minutes to set. Let cool.

3. To make the filling: Combine the sugar and butter in a large bowl. Beat until well blended. Beat in the eggs, one at a time, followed by the vanilla. Whisk together the flour and cocoa powder in a small bowl. Add to the wet mixture and stir until well blended. Spoon the mixture over the crust and bake for 35 minutes. While still warm, spread the marshmallow cream over the chocolate filling. Let cool completely.

4. To make the topping: Whisk together the sugar and cocoa powder in a medium bowl. Add the butter and stir to blend. Add the milk and vanilla and mix well to combine. Spread the topping evenly over the marshmallow cream. Garnish with the pecans, if using.

Steve Azar with his daughter, Ceilia

Terry Blackwood

TERRY BLACKWOOD is the son of Dole Blackwood, original founder of the famous Black-wood Brothers Quartet. He has been featured on many chart-topping singles while associated with the Imperials and Andrus Blackwood Company, and he has been a featured soloist on many Gaither Homecoming videos. Terry is currently singing selected dates with the Imperials. He also continues to perform as a soloist in many churches across the country. Terry, his wife, Tina, and their three children now make their home outside Nashville, Tennessee.

Terry Blackwood with his wife, Tina, and their children, Luke, Jesse, and Leah

MY FAVORITE CHRISTMAS memories come from time spent with my maternal grandparents, Grandmother and Grandfather Hawkins. Their old home place was located in a little community called Homewood, twelve miles out of Forest, Mississippi. My uncles and aunts and all their little ones visited at Christmastime. I played with my cousins until we were just ready to drop, and we ate until we thought our bellies would pop. Christmas in that rustic home was so special, sitting around the fire listening to all the old tales and snuggling into bed under a mountain of quilts to get warm. I remember that when I stood next to the bedroom wall, I felt the cold air coming in between the cracks in the boards.

Now Christmas is spent with my wife, Tina, and her family. There's a lot of laughter and poking fun at each other—such an enjoyable time. After opening our Christmas presents, we love watching home movies of Christmases past.

Every Christmas is unique in one way or another, and especially the year our son was baptized in Hawaii. No matter where you are, holidays are cherished times of families sharing food and fellowship.

Grandma's Southern Gospel Tea Cakes

My grandma made the best tea cakes. They were a special treat for us Blackwood boys during the holidays. I can just picture her hovering over her bowl in her kitchen making sure the ingredients were stirred in with a great big bunch of love. Now my wife and children enjoy the same tradition of baking these simple tea cakes at Christmas and sharing them with our family and friends. Just like Grandma used to bake. Makes 1 dozen

1 cup sugar
6 tablespoons ($^3/_4$ stick) unsalted butter
$^1/_4$ cup milk
1 large egg
$1^1/_2$ teaspoons vanilla extract
$2^1/_2$ cups unbleached, all-purpose flour, plus more for dusting
2 teaspoons baking powder

1. Preheat the oven to 350°F. Grease a baking sheet.

2. Place the sugar in a large bowl. Melt the butter in a small saucepan over low heat and add to the sugar. Stir to blend. Add the milk, egg, and vanilla and stir well to mix.

3. Whisk together the flour and baking powder. Add to the wet mixture and stir until it forms a moist dough. Turn out onto a clean work surface dusted with flour and gently pat into a $^1/_2$-inch-thick round. Using a 2-inch round cutter, cut out 12 cakes, re-rolling the scraps of dough as necessary, and place on the baking sheet. Bake for 10 minutes, or until golden and a wooden skewer inserted into the center of one cake comes out clean. Transfer to a wire rack to cool.

Pat Boone

*P*AT BOONE is fearless. For more than fifty years, he has been unafraid to try any style of music that was in vogue. From the smooth pop sounds of the early 1950s, through the rhythm and blues and rock and roll eras, to the hard rock and metal sounds of today, he has tried it all. His contribution to American culture has reached legendary status. With over forty-five million records sold, thirty-eight top-forty hits, and a string of successful movies and television appearances, Pat has established his place of honor in the minds and hearts of people all over the world.

Pat Boone with his wife, Shirley, and their children,
Laury, Debby, Lindy, and Cherry

ONE OF MY MOST poignant Christmas memories concerns my youngest daughter, Laury, and our big family grand piano. When Laury, wonderful, vibrant, and impulsive, at age eight asked Santa for a bicycle, Shirley and I were quick to oblige, as Santa's helpers. We bought the bike and put it out in our guest house under lock and key, to save until Christmas morning.

Meanwhile, when she was supposed to be practicing her piano lesson only two weeks before Christmas, Laury scratched her name in the veneer of the piano! When we discovered it, we were horrified, knowing it was there to stay—and there was no doubt about who had done it! We agonized over it, but had to finally tell a tearful Laury that no child who does something like that just before Christmas can expect to get her wish granted.

Christmas morning, when all the four daughters came into our big den where the Christmas stockings were hung near the Christmas tree, there were nice gifts in each of the stockings for each of the girls—but Laury's had a note from Santa in it. And it sadly explained why he couldn't bring her bicycle, though he had a beautiful one picked out for her, because she had scratched her name on the piano. I was videotaping her response, and wept behind the camera as Laury tearfully nodded affirmatively, "He's right—I don't deserve it."

Well, it took everything in us to hold off until Laury's birthday late in January, and then we told her that Santa had been impressed with her reaction Christmas morning, and rather than wait for the following December 25, he felt she should have it for her birthday. So all ended happily, and Laury learned a great lesson—and Shirley and I were just glad that her birthday came so soon after Christmas.

Old-Fashioned Christmas Shortbread

Serve this sweet shortbread and your guests will be writing you "Love Letters in the Sand!"
Makes 48 wedges

> 1 pound (4 sticks) unsalted butter
> 1 cup sugar
> 5 cups unbleached, all-purpose flour

1. Preheat the oven to 275°F. Lightly grease and flour four 8-inch round cake pans.

2. Combine the butter and sugar in a large bowl. Using electric beaters, beat the mixture on medium until it is light and fluffy. Beat in the flour, 1 cup at a time, until a soft dough forms.

3. Divide the dough into 4 pieces and press each piece over the bottom of each prepared cake pan to form a smooth, even layer. Prick the top of the dough with a fork in several places to let the steam escape. Bake for 45 to 55 minutes or until the shortbread is pale brown. Let cool for 10 minutes. Remove the shortbread from each pan and cut into wedges with a sharp knife.

Roy Clark

ROY CLARK has done it all. In the 1970s, he symbolized country music in the United States and abroad, using his musical talent and entertaining personality to bring country music into homes around the world. For more than twenty years, he co-hosted the enormously successful television show *Hee Haw*. His talents are multiple, including proficiency in guitar, banjo, and mandolin. As a vocalist, he has enjoyed a string of hits, including such songs as "Tip of My Fingers," "Yesterday, When I Was Young," and "Thank God and Greyhound." His consistency as an exciting entertainer and his success as a businessman have made Roy a country music icon and one of America's favorite performers.

MY LIFE CHANGED when I was thirteen years old. I remember the exact moment. My neighbor had a Harmony arch-top guitar and one day he let me hold it. It was the first time I ever held an instrument that had six strings. I ran a pick down them and heard a sound I'd never heard before and decided instantly that I had to learn to play it!

That fall I got out Mama's old Sears catalog and circled the guitar I liked the best. When Christmas morning finally came I ran downstairs with my heart pounding. Sure enough, there it was under the Christmas tree along with a copy of *Smith's Three Hundred Chords for Guitar.* I grabbed them both and ran up to my room, closed the door, and started playing. In fact, I played for so long that my fingers swelled up and I had to dip them in a glass of ice water to ease the pain—but I kept right on playing.

My daddy was a great teacher, and two weeks after Christmas I was good enough to play my first gig with him at a local dance!

I'm a Pickin' Scrumptious Sweet Potato Pie

Take it from me, or ask any one of my *Hee Haw* friends about my sweet potato pie. It's a real crust above the rest! Makes one 9-inch pie

3 cups hot cooked mashed sweet potatoes
4 tablespoons (1/2 stick) unsalted butter
2 large eggs
1/4 cup evaporated milk
1 1/2 cups firmly packed light brown sugar
2 teaspoons ground cinnamon
1 teaspoon grated nutmeg
1/2 teaspoon salt
1 (9-inch) unbaked pie crust

1. Preheat the oven to 350°F.

2. Place the sweet potatoes and butter in a large bowl. Stir until blended. Beat in the eggs, one at a time, followed by the evaporated milk.

3. Whisk together the sugar, cinnamon, nutmeg, and salt in a medium bowl. Add to the sweet potato mixture and stir until well blended. Pour into the unbaked pie crust and bake the pie for 45 minutes or until the center is set. Let cool on a wire rack before serving.

Carol Lee Cooper

CAROL LEE COOPER, the daughter of *Grand Ole Opry*'s star Wilma Lee and the late Stoney Cooper, has enjoyed a diversified career. She has hosted her own radio show, interviewing such legends as Andy Griffith, Dolly Parton, Gene Autry, and Garth Brooks. She has directed Charles Dickens's *A Christmas Carol* for the *Grand Ole Opry* with many of country music's biggest stars. She formed a group called the Carol Lee Singers and has performed with just about every star that graces the *Grand Ole Opry* stage. The group has appeared in movies, commercials, network shows, and television specials and has performed for ambassadors, vice presidents, and even presidents.

Carol Lee Cooper with Elvis Presley

CHRISTMAS IS MY FAVORITE time of the year. I love the bright lights and beautiful decorations, but I always long for a white Christmas. I grew up in West Virginia, and we always had gorgeous white Christmases there.

Many special events have taken place at the *Grand Ole Opry,* but I remember one particular Christmas event that happened there when I was fifteen years old. The word came trickling through the Opry halls that Elvis was in the building. Someone said that a girl had already passed out when she met him, and I remember thinking, "That's not going to happen to me."

My mother and dad and I were waiting our turn to rehearse for the show while Bill Monroe was rehearsing his song, and in walked Elvis dressed in a tuxedo. He was extremely handsome and very polite. He said hello to everyone, came over to me and my family, and introduced himself. He came back over to me and talked a minute, then said, "Let's dance." When I told him I couldn't dance, he just grabbed my hand, and we started dancing to Bill Monroe's "Blue Moon of Kentucky." Now folks, it just doesn't get any better than that—dancing with Elvis as Bill Monroe, the father of bluegrass music, sings "Blue Moon of Kentucky"!

As Elvis got ready to leave, he bent down and kissed me on the cheek. Then he looked at my dad and said, "Can I take her home?" My dad looked at him kindly and said with a smile, "Not this time," and Elvis left. Although I didn't pass out during my encounter with Elvis, it was certainly an incredible experience.

Years later I was told that one of Elvis's bodyguards told a WSM air personality in an interview that Elvis left the Opry that night to go to the governor's mansion, and he kept saying, "I've got to go back and find that Carol Lee Cooper."

Sing for Your Supper Blueberry Strawberry Surprise

This is the dessert my husband loves. I hope you will love it, too! Makes one 9-inch pie

- 1 (8-ounce) package cream cheese, softened
- 1 (4-ounce) box instant lemon pudding and pie filling mix
- 1 cup milk
- 2 teaspoons grated lemon zest
- 2 cups whipped topping, such as Cool Whip
- 1 (9-inch) prepared graham cracker pie crust
- 1 cup sliced fresh strawberries
- 1 cup fresh blueberries

1. Combine the cream cheese, pudding mix, milk, and lemon zest in a large bowl. Beat until the mixture is creamy and smooth. Gently stir or fold in 1 cup of the whipping topping until it is incorporated. Spoon the filling into the prepared pie crust and cover with the remaining 1 cup of whipped topping. Chill in the refrigerator for 4 hours to set.

2. Just before serving, garnish the pie with the fresh strawberries and blueberries.

Billy Ray Cyrus

$\mathcal{B}$ILLY RAY CYRUS is definitely living the American dream. There are very few singers who are lucky enough to have the first song they release take them on a magic carpet ride of the magnitude that Billy Ray has experienced. That song, "Achy Breaky Heart," plus his good looks, catapulted him onto the music scene, selling nine million CDs and making him a household name. "Achy Breaky Heart" became a line-dancing anthem in 1992. He has received many awards, including Humanitarian of the Year for his tireless philanthropic work. He was cast in the weekly PAX TV show *Doc,* playing a Montana doctor who moves to New York City.

MY CHILDHOOD was not an easy time financially for my mother and our family; and especially at Christmas, it was difficult to get the bills paid and give gifts to the members of our family. I remember one Christmas in particular when I was a senior in high school. It had been a rough year financially, and my mother had been forced to sell her mother's piano just to get by and take care of us kids. I decided to surprise her, so I used all the money I had saved to buy her a used piano that I had found for sale. I believe that I will always consider that Christmas as the most memorable for me, because I fully understood the true meaning of giving at Christmas. That memory has truly influenced the way that my wife and children celebrate the holidays.

This past Christmas, we delivered clothing to families in need in the coal mines in Appalachia. There is a wonderful organization called Appalachian Mission of Hope, and they help out many families all year round, and especially at Christmastime. If you visit the Billy Ray Cyrus Web site, there is a link to this great group of people.

In our home, we always have a real tree at Christmas—it just wouldn't be the same without one. We decorate the tree with the same sentimental ornaments every year, but every year my wife, Tish, gets the kids a new Christmas ornament to use the following year. Sometimes we gather around the tree when we are finished decorating it and sing our favorite Christmas songs, "Silent Night" and "Away in a Manger." Every Christmas Eve we celebrate the candlelight service at church; and last year I sang with my daughter Brandi for her first time in front of the congregation—it was very special.

Christmas Day morning last year was so exciting for the kids, because they had wanted a trampoline for a long time, and we surprised them with one. To make our day complete, our Christmas dinner was centered around a huge turkey—my favorite holiday treat!

Christmas is all about giving, and I don't think that you can fully receive that warm holiday feeling unless you share your time and gifts with others who are less fortunate.

Achy Breaky Cake

Simple pleasures are the best! My family enjoys the cake made from this simple recipe, especially during the holiday season. It's a special treat from our house to yours, and it is sure to be a hit at your Christmas dinner. **Serves 6**

1 (18.25-ounce) package yellow cake mix

1 (14-ounce) can condensed milk

1 (6-ounce) bottle caramel
   sauce, such as Hershey's

1 (16-ounce) container whipped topping, such as
   Cool Whip

2 (2.1-ounce) Butterfinger candy bars, crushed

1. Preheat the oven to 350°F. Grease a 13 by 9-inch baking dish.

2. Prepare the cake according to package directions. Bake, and let cool slightly.

3. Whisk together the condensed milk and caramel sauce in a small bowl. Using a wooden skewer, poke numerous holes over the top of the warm cake. Pour the caramel mixture over the cake and let it seep in; poke more holes as necessary until the mixture has been absorbed. Let the cake cool completely.

4. Spread the whipped topping over the cooled cake and garnish with the crushed candy bars. Refrigerate until ready to serve.

Billy Ray Cyrus with his wife, Tish, and their children, Noah, Miley, Brasion, and Trace

Charlie Daniels

ORN IN 1936 in Wilmington, North Carolina, Charlie Daniels was raised on a musical diet that included gospel, bluegrass, rhythm and blues, and country music. After graduating from high school in 1955, already skilled on guitar, fiddle, and mandolin, Charlie formed a rock-'n'-roll band and hit the road. In 1969, Charlie moved to Nashville to work as a session guitarist. He broke through as a record maker himself in 1973 with the hit song titled "Uneasy Rider." During the 1970s, he continued his string of hits, which included the perennial favorite "The Devil Went Down to Georgia." Charlie and his wife, Hazel, continue to live in Nashville, Tennessee.

Charlie Daniels with his wife, Hazel

I HOPE I NEVER GROW UP so much that I can't get that kid kind of feeling about Christmas. I love colored lights and mistletoe and red candles and packages wrapped up with ribbons and bows. I love "White Christmas" and "Silent Night" and candy canes and holly branches and snuggling close to Hazel in front of the fireplace. I love watching my son open his presents on Christmas morning. I love having our friends over on Christmas Eve night. I love our employees' Christmas party with Santa Claus for the little ones and Christmas bonus checks for the big ones. I love turkey and dressing and pumpkin pie and hugging everybody as they come through the door. I just love Christmas, and most of all I love the absolute fact that Jesus Christ would leave the unspeakable splendor of Heaven to come to this earth and give his life for sinners like me. In the wonderful words of Tiny Tim, "God bless us every one." A Merry Christmas to all!

Southern Boy's Wonderful Sugar Cookies

This is a recipe that we've made at Christmastime with our son every year for thirty years. It truly is a family tradition! Of course, you can make them at any holiday and use the appropriate cookie cutters for the occasion. Makes 2 dozen

1½ cups confectioner's sugar
½ pound (2 sticks) unsalted butter, softened
1 large egg
1½ teaspoons vanilla extract
2½ cups unbleached, all-purpose flour, plus more
    for dusting
1 teaspoon baking soda
1 teaspoon cream of tartar
Colored sugar for sprinkling

1. Combine the confectioner's sugar and butter in a large bowl and blend until smooth. Mix in the egg and vanilla. Whisk together the flour, baking soda, and cream of tartar in a medium bowl. Add to the wet ingredients and stir well to blend. Seal the bowl with plastic wrap and refrigerate for 3 hours to chill.

2. Preheat the oven to 375°F. Coat a baking sheet with nonstick cooking spray.

3. On a clean work surface dusted with flour, roll out half of the dough to a ¼-inch thickness. Cut out designs with one or more cookie cutters and, working in batches, place the cookies on the prepared pan. Sprinkle with the colored sugar and bake for 7 to 8 minutes or until golden. Let the cookies cool slightly before transferring to wire racks to cool completely. Finish making the rest of the cookies in this manner, rerolling the scraps of dough as necessary.

Dan Truman

DAN TRUMAN is the piano player in the highly successful country group Diamond Rio. The group began its climb to stardom as the Tennessee River Boys, playing at the Opryland USA theme park in Nashville in the 1980s. In 1989, they became Diamond Rio. The following year, they signed with Arista Records and throughout the decade had a continuing stream of number one hits. Their chart success earned four Country Music Association awards for the vocal group. In 1998, they were inducted into the *Grand Ole Opry*, the first band in fourteen years to receive that honor. Today, the band continues producing one hit song after another.

YOU MUST TRY ONE of our favorite holiday traditions—apple pudding. When we cook it and smell it, it's instantly Christmas! This recipe came from an old family friend. Most pudding recipes like this one call for putting it into a can and then putting that in a bigger pan filled with hot water and steaming the whole thing. This apple pudding recipe is simpler, because you only have to put it in the pan and bake it; yet, you get the same moist, cakey results as you do with the more complicated recipes. I'm sure that helped make it such a hit. The Truman family likes to cook, which is why Christmas memories at our house are all about baking together. Have fun trying this yummy family tradition.

Something Cool Apple Pudding

This is one of our favorite holiday desserts. The smell of the grated apples and wonderful spices fills our kitchens during the holidays. This dessert has also become a must-have at the annual Diamond Rio Christmas party. **Serves 6**

Pudding

1 cup sugar

$^1/_2$ cup vegetable oil

1 large egg

1 cup unbleached, all-purpose flour

1 teaspoon baking soda

$^1/_2$ teaspoon ground cinnamon

$^1/_2$ teaspoon grated nutmeg

$^1/_4$ teaspoon salt

2 cups grated peeled apples

$^1/_2$ cup chopped nuts, such as walnuts

Sauce

8 tablespoons (1 stick) unsalted butter

$^1/_2$ cup sugar

$^1/_2$ cup evaporated milk

$1^1/_2$ teaspoons ground cinnamon

$^1/_2$ teaspoon grated nutmeg

1. Preheat the oven to 350°F. Grease a 3-quart casserole.

2. **To make the pudding:** Combine the sugar, oil, and egg in a large bowl. Stir well to blend. Whisk together the flour, baking soda, cinnamon, nutmeg, and salt in a small bowl. Add to the wet mixture and stir well to combine. Stir in the apples and nuts, along with 2 tablespoons of hot water. Trans-fer to the prepared casserole and bake for 45 to 55 minutes, or until puffed and golden.

3. **To make the sauce:** Melt the butter in a small saucepan over medium heat. Add the sugar, evaporated milk, cinnamon, and nutmeg and cook, stirring often, until the mixture has turned transparent, about 10 minutes. Spoon the warm sauce over each serving of pudding.

Dan Truman (top row, far left) with Diamond Rio

Jeff Foxworthy

JUST SAY THE PHRASE, "You might be a redneck if . . ." and Jeff Foxworthy immediately comes to mind. He has sold more comedy recordings than any artist in history. He has been nominated for Grammy Awards numerous times, and he is the best-selling author of eleven books. Jeff stars in and produces the television series *Blue Collar TV* on the WB network. His comedy films are top DVD/VHS sellers; millions have been sold. He has an HBO special and two Showtime specials to his credit.

Jeff Foxworthy with his wife, Gregg, and their children, Jules and Jordan

ONE OF MY FAVORITE and funniest holiday moments happened a few years ago, when the cat climbed up in our Christmas tree and knocked it over. We sure do miss that cat.

My wife filled the house with Christmas music for weeks before the big day. The CD player ran continuously, playing every Christmas song imaginable. I threatened to jump off a bridge if I heard "Grandma Got Run Over by a Reindeer" one more time.

My favorite song is "O Holy Night" by Martina McBride. Bring me some Kleenex; I always cry when I hear it. Of course, the kids enjoy laughing at their sappy dad. Part of the Foxworthy family tradition to celebrate the season is to spend Christmas Eve at church. I cry when we sing the Christmas carols.

On Christmas morning for the past few years, we have treated the whole family to brunch at the Ritz-Carlton Hotel. There are about twenty-five to thirty of us, and we're way too loud. And usually some snooty customer asks for his money back.

My fans have been so faithful in supporting me and my family, and we love to return that love. We haven't always been as blessed as we have been in recent years, and we know that Christmas isn't the same in a home without gifts, especially for the children. We really enjoy giving back to those in our area, so during the Christmas season we carry gifts to the Community Charity Center. It is part of our Christmas joy to provide gifts and a trip for the children at the Georgia Sheriffs' Youth Home.

Christmas is a special time to my family, and we enjoy helping make it a special time for others. Merry Christmas to all!

Redneck Paw Paw's Pecan Pie

You don't have to be a redneck to enjoy this Fox-worthy holiday favorite. Makes one 8-inch pie

3 large eggs
1 cup sugar
$\frac{1}{4}$ cup light corn syrup
2 tablespoons unbleached, all-purpose flour
1 teaspoon vanilla extract
1 cup pecans, chopped
1 (8-inch) unbaked pie crust

1. Preheat the oven to 325°F.

2. Place the eggs in a large bowl and beat until well blended. Add the sugar, corn syrup, flour, and vanilla and beat until creamy and smooth. Stir in the pecans and pour into the pie crust. Bake for 40 to 45 minutes, or until the filling is firm to the touch. Let cool on a wire rack before cutting into slices.

Janie Fricke

JANIE FRICKE says that all she ever wanted to do is sing, and to be sure, she got her wish. From a farm in Indiana she gravitated to Memphis, Dallas, and Los Angeles, where she became the voice on advertising jingles for such companies as United Airlines, Red Lobster, 7-Up, and Coca-Cola. This led her to singing backup on recordings by such country music greats as Loretta Lynn, Eddie Rabbit, Ronnie Milsap, Charlie Rich, Barbara Mandrell, and Elvis Presley. Duets with Johnny Duncan, Merle Haggard, and Moe Bandy led to her first major solo recording contract. She soon had smash hits, such as "Don't Worry 'Bout Me Baby," "He's a Heartache," and "Your Heart's Not in It." Country Music Association's Female Vocalist of the Year, Music City News's Female Vocalist of the Year, Billboard's Top Country Female Vocalist, and Academy Country Female Vocalist of the Year are just a few of the outstanding awards presented to her for her great vocal talents.

ONE OF MY EARLIEST special memories of Christmas is going to church on Christmas Eve as a child. My dad's church was the Lutheran church in Fort Wayne, Indiana. After the service, we would embark on a thirty-mile ride back to our farm. My sister and I would sit in the car and wait as my parents would go in and see if the coast was clear and that Santa Claus had gone back up the chimney and left us our gifts. Of course, we had left cookies and milk for Santa, and we were thrilled to see they had disappeared.

The biggest thrill was opening the presents, but equal to that was decorating the Christmas tree. My mother would get out the boxes and boxes of special sentimental ornaments handed down through the family for generations. It was the same routine each year, but it was always as exciting as if it were the first time.

Today, it is a little different because I don't live near any of my family. I have never had children, so I don't really have a family where I live. It is just my husband, Jeff, and me. So during the holidays we spend a lot of time traveling to be with different members of our family. No matter which family we are with at Christmas, there is always a big dinner: ham or turkey, salads, and all of the desserts. My family loves to fix pies. One of Mom's traditional pies was a mincemeat pie from scratch. She would first cook up the beef and then add all the raisins and brown sugar. We put a hot brandy or hot rum sauce over it. I can almost smell the aroma from Mom's kitchen. Since Mom can't cook anymore, my sister prepares it Mom's way.

Then at home in Dallas, we do most of our holiday singing at church. We attend all the Christmas services. On Christmas Day, however, for me, home with family is truly where my heart is.

Don't Worry 'Bout Me Mincemeat Pie

Don't worry about what to make this year for the holidays. This is a winner, every time.
Makes 15 cups of filling for three 9-inch pies

  1 (3-pound) rump roast
  7½ cups diced unpeeled apples
  5 cups sugar
  3 cups cider vinegar
  2½ cups diced suet
  2½ cups whole raisins
  1½ cups finely chopped raisins
  ³/₄ pound (about 1½ cups) citron, finely chopped
  1 cup molasses
  ½ cup white vinegar
  2 tablespoons ground cinnamon
  2 tablespoons ground cloves
  2 tablespoons ground allspice
  2 whole nutmegs, grated
  1 tablespoon ground mace
  2 tablespoons lemon extract
  1 tablespoon almond extract
  2 oranges
  2 lemons

  1½ cups brandy
  Salt, to taste
  6 (9-inch) unbaked pie crusts
  Flour for dusting

1. Place the rump roast in a soup pot and fill the pot with enough water to come two thirds of the way up the meat. Bring the mixture to a boil, reduce the heat to low, and simmer the meat for 3 hours, or until it is falling apart and tender. Save 3 cups of the beef simmering liquid, then drain the roast. When the meat has cooled, chop it into small dice.

2. Transfer the meat back to the soup pot and add the 3 cups of reserved liquid. Add the apples, sugar, cider vinegar, suet, whole raisins, chopped raisins, citron, molasses, white vinegar, cinnamon, cloves, allspice, grated nutmeg, mace, and lemon and almond extracts.

3. Grate the zest from both oranges and lemons and set aside. Squeeze the juice from the oranges and lemons and add to the pot. Bring the mincemeat to a boil, reduce the heat to low, and simmer the mixture for 1½ hours. Stir in the orange and lemon zest and the brandy and season with salt to taste. Let cool.

4. Preheat the oven to 350°F.

5. To assemble the pies, line the bottom of 3 pie plates with one crust each. Lightly dust a clean work surface with flour and gently roll out each remaining crust so that it forms a flat disc large enough to cover each generously heaped pie.

6. Divide the mincemeat filling among the three pies and cover each with a top crust. Using your fingers or the tines of a fork, gently press down along the outer edges of the dough to seal the crusts. Using a sharp knife, make several small slits in the top crust to let the steam escape. Bake the pies for 35 minutes or until the crusts are golden. Let cool on wire racks before serving warm or at room temperature.

Amy Grant

AMY GRANT's story is straight out of Hollywood. Her transition from sweeping floors in a Nashville recording studio at the age of seventeen to becoming one of the music world's greatest icons is the stuff movies are made of. Her first album, *Amy Grant,* was an instant hit. Contemporary Christian music was growing and Amy became the leader. In 1982, she won her first Dove Awards, including Contemporary Album of the Year and Artist of the Year, plus a Grammy for Best Gospel Performance. Amy broke through the crossover barrier with "Baby, Baby," making her a mainstream pop star. "Baby, Baby" was the first Christian music song to reach the coveted number one spot on *Billboard*'s pop chart. Amy is married to country music superstar Vince Gill. They reside in Nashville, Tennessee, with their children.

Amy Grant with her husband, Vince Gill

ONE OF MY MOST vivid memories of Christmas as a little girl is of my father shooting mistletoe down from the trees on our farm. We would gather the fallen mistletoe and hang it in our house. We would also have a big Christmas breakfast instead of the traditional dinner. The whole family would gather in the kitchen while the bacon, eggs, and sausage were cooking. Breakfast is easier to make than dinner, which allowed us to spend less time cooking and more time enjoying each other's company. One of my favorite Christmas morning dishes is cheese grits, but I also love fruit cobbler and pancakes. My advice is to make whatever you want—just do it together and don't be afraid to dole out jobs. My youngest, Corrina, likes cracking the eggs.

House of Love Christmas Pizza

Christmas pizza is a welcome treat around our house. The ingredients are family favorites: chocolate, nuts, cherries, and coconut, all rolled into this one-of-a-kind dessert. Everybody loves it. To bring extra smiles and family fun during the holidays, enjoy this scrumptious pizza. **Serves 8**

1 cup white chocolate chips
1 cup semisweet chocolate chips
1/2 cup salted roasted peanuts
1/2 cup mini marshmallows
1/2 cup crispy rice cereal, such as Rice Crispies
1/2 cup sweetened shredded coconut
1/4 cup red candied cherries
1/4 cup green candied cherries

1. Coat a 10-inch pizza pan with nonstick cooking spray.

2. Combine 3/4 cup of the white chocolate chips with the semisweet chocolate chips in the top of a double boiler over medium heat. Cook, stirring occasionally, until the chips are melted. Stir in the peanuts, marshmallows, and cereal and pour into the prepared pizza pan. Spread the mixture evenly across the surface. Scatter the coconut over the "pizza" and gently press the cherries on top.

3. Melt the remaining 1/4 cup of white chocolate chips in the top of a double boiler and drizzle over the pizza. Chill in the refrigerator until firm.

George Jones

A NATIVE OF SARATOGA, Texas, George Jones grew up singing for tips. But in 1954 when he recorded his own song, "Why, Baby, Why," he launched a career that has been the definition of legendary. With more charted singles than any other artist in popular music, George is one of American music's most respected and honored entertainers. With a unique vocal style and colorful personality, "The Possum" continues to delight fans by producing new records and performing more than a hundred concerts a year.

I GREW UP VERY POOR and have to say that I don't have too many good memories of Christmas as a child. But as an adult, I have great Christmases every year, seeing the wonder in children's eyes when they come to my farm and see the thousands of lights and decorations all over the farm and the house. We might not get much snow around here, but we do our best to make sure that at our place, it's truly a Christmas wonderland.

People come from miles and miles away to see the display. One night we invite Mr. and Mrs. Santa Claus to join us there, so the kids can visit with them. It gives me so much joy to do this for our friends and fans. Of course, my greatest source of pleasure comes from seeing my grandchildren on Christmas morning when they find what Santa has brought them. It is total chaos, but we love it. That is truly the joy of Christmas for me.

My favorite song is "Here Comes Santa Claus." I sing it many times every year, and my grandchildren gather around me and sing along. That makes them get even more excited about the arrival of jolly ol' Santa.

For our Christmas meal, you name it, and we have it. My wife, Nancy, fixes the entire feast. She cooks turkey, ham, and all the fixings. My favorite is Cajun rice as only Nancy can fix it, and the red velvet cake she bakes is the best I have ever had. So, how many more days 'til Christmas?

Possum's Red Velvet Cake

For many, red velvet cake is a Southern Christmas tradition; it sure is at the Jones house! Here is one Christmas treat that is as good to look at as it is to eat. Serves 16

Cake

$1\frac{1}{2}$ cups sugar

$1\frac{1}{2}$ cups vegetable oil

1 cup buttermilk

2 large eggs

1 tablespoon red food coloring

1 teaspoon white vinegar

$2\frac{1}{2}$ cups unbleached, all-purpose flour

1 tablespoon unsweetened cocoa powder

1 teaspoon baking soda

Topping

1 (1-pound) box confectioner's sugar

12 ounces cream cheese, softened

6 tablespoons (³/₄ stick) margarine, softened

1 teaspoon vanilla extract

1¹/₂ cups chopped pecans

1. Preheat the oven to 350°F. Grease and flour three 8-inch round cake pans.

2. To make the cake: Combine the sugar, oil, and buttermilk in a large bowl. Beat until well blended. Beat in the eggs, red food coloring, and vinegar. Whisk together the flour, cocoa, and baking soda in a medium bowl. Add to the wet ingredients and stir until mixed. Divide the batter among the prepared pans and bake the cakes for 35 minutes, or until a wooden skewer inserted into the center of one cake comes out clean. Let the cakes cool in the pans for several minutes before inverting onto wire racks to cool completely.

3. To make the topping: Combine the sugar, cream cheese, margarine, and vanilla in a large bowl. Using electric beaters, blend until the icing is creamy and smooth. Place one of the cakes, puffed side up, on a decorative plate. Spread a thin layer of icing over the top of the cake. Place a second cake, in the same manner, over the first layer and spread a thin layer of icing over the top. Place the last cake, in the same manner, over the second layer. Add the pecans to the remaining icing and frost the sides and top of the entire cake.

George Jones with his wife, Nancy

Gordon Stoker

GORDON STOKER is the longest-standing member of a music group that has sold more than 2.6 billion recordings. The most-recorded singing group in the world, the Jordanaires have backed up hundreds of artists, including such industry giants as Patsy Cline, Jim Reeves, Ricky Nelson, and Elvis Presley. Gordon started his career as a piano player before he was even a teenager. At age fifteen, he became the youngest musician on the *Grand Ole Opry;* and in 1950, he joined the Jordanaires, singing tenor.

🌲 🌲 🌲 🌲 🌲

The original Jordanaires: Neal Matthews Jr., Gordon Stoker, Hoyt Hawkins, and Ray Walker with Elvis Presley

THERE WAS A WHOLE LOT of music and singing at Christmas in our house because my parents, my sister, my two brothers, and I all played instruments. Of course, we loved Christmas carols and loved singing traditional Christmas songs in church. I can remember the first time I heard the "Hallelujah Chorus" by Handel. It was without question the most heavenly music I had ever heard. Our church didn't have a choir with enough members to pull off this masterpiece, so my first exposure to it was through the radio. I knew if I could hear angels singing, it would sound like it did that night. When I was in college, I had the opportunity to sing all of Handel's *Messiah* with the college choir. What a thrill that was!

In addition to music, my mother would make the season special by baking some of the most incredible holiday foods. My favorites were the cakes. She would usually bake banana, raisin, chocolate, pineapple, and coconut cakes. My sister-in-law would bake a fruit cake, and believe me—it was the best I have ever eaten. When I got older I learned why it was so good—she soaked it in wine! Although we had cakes throughout the year, we never had the choices we did at Christmas. On Christmas Eve, my father would bring in a large box filled with candies, fruit, and so many good things, I'm getting hungry just thinking about those days.

The first Christmas tree I remember had a set of eight lights. It certainly wouldn't make much of a showing these days, but it looked like heaven to me as a child. It was the centerpiece to my most special Christmas memory—the year I got my first train. I'll never forget peeping the night before Christmas and seeing my mom and brother setting the train on its track at the dining room table. It had three coach cars and one coal car. The engine had a little light on the front powered by a battery in the coal car. I still have some parts of that train set.

Walk Them Golden Stairs Cheesecake

The Jordanaires were a favorite of Elvis, and during his early years in the business he included them in his recordings and movies. Cheesecake was one of the special desserts they would bring on the bus for road trips. A homemade cheesecake would taste great after a concert and was a touch of home. Serves 6 to 8

1 (8-ounce) package cream cheese, softened
1/3 cup sugar, or Splenda to make a reduced-sugar cheesecake
1 tablespoon vanilla extract
1 cup sour cream
1 cup whipped topping, such as Cool Whip
1 (9-inch) prepared graham cracker pie crust

Combine the cream cheese, sugar, and vanilla in a large bowl and beat until creamy and smooth. Using a rubber spatula, fold in the sour cream, followed by the whipped topping. Transfer the mixture to the prepared graham cracker pie crust and chill in the refrigerator for several hours to set.

Naomi Judd

MOMMA JUDD, as Naomi is lovingly referred to by her friends in the music business, thinks of herself as a communicator. Whether writing a book, a song, or singing and acting, she says that finding a way to share common experiences is her grand passion. As half of country music's most famous mother–daughter team, Naomi captured national attention during the duo's meteoric rise, which includes twenty top-ten hits, five Grammys, and a multitude of industry awards. Naomi's bout with hepatitis C brought the Judds' reign at the top to an end. Today she is completely cured of the virus and spends her time speaking, writing books, and spending her energy on humanitarian activities, social issues, and personal-growth education.

ONE OF MY MOST memorable holidays was the year we "took back Christmas." We got a group of friends together and went to an inner-city church in Nashville, where we helped prepare a hearty holiday dinner for twenty-four homeless people. We gave them warm clothes, sang carols, and visited. The next day, we went to a center for terminally ill children, giving them presents and refreshments and singing their favorite Christmas songs. When we returned home, we looked like anything but the "perfect designer family." The two days made us reflect on our own blessings, and we felt we had acknowledged the reason for the season.

We've been conditioned to feel we have to give gifts for special occasions. This winds up being more for ourselves to avoid guilt than for the recipient of the gift. If you find a special gift and have a creative urge, go ahead and give the gift. Otherwise, make it honest. If you can, give a present of words; talk to someone about how much he or she means to you, give thanks, share memories, offer affirmations, make handmade items, go to an event with this person and share the experience together, give blood, offer to babysit for an over-

worked mother, give new books to the library, help a neighbor in need, take some groceries to a food shelter, do volunteer work at a local soup kitchen or women's shelter.

Christmas and other holidays can be either a chore or a treasure. You always have a choice.

Love Can Build a Bridge Texas Lizzies

These delicious festive cookies are almost like tiny, tiny fruitcakes. Baking cookies together is one of our oldest family traditions. Wy, Ashley, and I bake batches of them Christmas Eve and deliver them to our local sheriff's department. I urge you to teach your kids to respect our law-enforcement officials as well as our teachers, clergy, and the elderly. Makes 9 dozen

8 tablespoons (1 stick) unsalted butter, softened
1 (1-pound) box light brown sugar
4 large eggs
3½ cups unbleached, all-purpose flour

1 tablespoon baking soda

1 teaspoon ground cinnamon

1 teaspoon grated nutmeg

3/4 cup whiskey

1 (15-ounce) box golden raisins

1 1/4 cups dark raisins

1 cup chopped candied red cherries

1 cup chopped candied green cherries

1/2 cup chopped walnuts

1/2 cup chopped pecans

1. Preheat the oven to 350°F. Grease several baking sheets.

2. Place the butter in a large bowl. Using electric beaters, beat the butter for 2 minutes. Add the sugar and beat until the mixture is light and fluffy, about 1 minute. Beat in the eggs, one at a time.

3. Whisk together the flour, baking soda, cinnamon, and nutmeg in a medium bowl. Add one third of this mixture to the wet ingredients, along with 1/4 cup of the whiskey. Beat the mixture on low speed until well blended. Repeat the process two more times with the remaining flour mixture and whiskey. Stir in the raisins, cherries, and nuts.

4. Using a generous 1 tablespoon of dough as your measure, drop portions of dough on a prepared baking sheet 2 inches apart. Bake the cookies for 10 to 12 minutes, or until puffed and lightly browned. Transfer to wire racks to cool. Continue making cookies in this manner until you have used up all the dough.

Naomi Judd with her husband, Larry Strickland

Buddy Killen

A NATIVE OF FLORENCE, Alabama, Buddy Killen became part of Nashville's music community less than twenty-four hours after his high school graduation. He began his career as a bass player on the *Grand Ole Opry,* and "picked" on the road for such big stars as Jim Reeves, Ray Price, and Hank Williams Sr. Buddy became one of the world's foremost country music publishers, in addition to being a top-ranked restaurateur and business entrepreneur. He's an award-winning songwriter, highly acclaimed record producer, singer, actor, and author. Buddy resides in Nashville, Tennessee, with his wife, Carolyn.

Buddy Killen and his wife, Carolyn, with their bird Scratch

MY MOTHER AND FATHER worked long hours in Killen's Café, a little meat and three, which they owned and ran in Florence, Alabama. My late brother, Burt; my sisters Joyce, June, and Mary; and I were all left to find a source of entertainment. The Christmas I was eight, we decided to take matters into our own hands. We found a hatchet and went into some nearby woods to fetch a cedar tree, which I'm sure was loaded with ticks. We took a two-by-four and built a base to hold the tree upright. I can still smell the aroma of the popcorn, which we strung together by using a needle and thread to make a strand as part of our tree decoration. We pinched off little dabs of cotton and threw them all over the tree. We had no fancy decorations, so everything was makeshift. But we didn't care. We had our very own Christmas tree.

Then the real fun started. We had a taffy pull. In my day, any enterprising young person knew how to make fudge or taffy. So we did both. The fudge was boring. But then came the taffy. I'm sure you can imagine what havoc five unsupervised youngsters can create with stringy, sticky taffy as it is stretched from room to room, sticking to everything in its path. Thank goodness we had loving, understanding parents or today I might not be here to share my favorite Christmas memories.

We Love Each Other Chocolate Fudge

Most families have their own version of homemade fudge. Carolyn and I are no different. After a day of skiing we love to cozy up to a warm fireplace with our favorite hot drink and a fudge square or two. Try it; you'll like our spin on this holiday delight. **Makes 2 pounds**

4 cups sugar
1 (12-ounce) can evaporated milk
2 teaspoons vanilla extract
1 (7-ounce) jar marshmallow cream
8 tablespoons (1 stick) unsalted butter, softened
1 (12-ounce) package semisweet chocolate chips
3 ounces semisweet chocolate, chopped
2$\frac{1}{2}$ cups chopped pecans

1. Coat a 13 by 9-inch baking dish with nonstick cooking spray.

2. Combine the sugar and evaporated milk in a large saucepan. Stir to blend and bring to a boil over medium-high heat. Continue cooking the mixture until it reaches the soft-ball stage on a candy thermometer. Remove from the heat and stir in the vanilla.

3. Stir in the marshmallow cream and butter, then blend in the chocolate chips and chopped chocolate. Continue stirring until the mixture is creamy and smooth. Stir in the pecans and pour the fudge into the prepared baking dish. Chill in the refrigerator for at least 8 hours to set. When ready to eat, cut into small squares.

Duane Propes

LITTLE TEXAS debuted on the charts in 1991 with the song "Some Guys Have All the Luck"—but not before performing on the road over three hundred days a year for three long years. Once Lady Luck smiled on them, the group followed up hit after hit with top-ten songs such as "First Time for Everything," "My Love," "What Might Have Been," and the still-popular "God Blessed Texas." With a string of hits and a load of awards under their belts, Little Texas continues to traverse the country, performing night after night, and is still known as one of the hardest-working bands in country music.

MY FAVORITE Christmas memory is one from a Christmas Eve we spent at my grandmother's house in Millville, Texas. It was a rare occurrence because we always held the family Christmas at our house. I'm not sure how old I was, but I was reading well enough for my mother to ask me to read the Christmas story from *The Children's Bible* to the family—my parents, my grandparents, and my great-grandparents.

To that point, Santa Claus had been the most important part of Christmas to me. But as I read the story aloud, it suddenly dawned on me that Jesus was the real focal point of the entire celebration. The toys were forgotten as the realization of everything I had been taught in Sunday school came flooding back to me in a wave of true consciousness. Here we were celebrating the birth of the son of God by giving each other gifts. As I read the passages, I suddenly knew that the real gift of Christmas was God's gift of His only son, Jesus Christ. It made such an impression on me at the time that I know I'll never forget that Christmas.

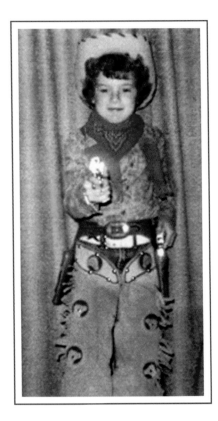

Kickin' East Texas Black-Bottom Cupcakes

One of my fondest memories of growing up in East Texas is that of going to my grandparents' house for Sunday dinner and special holiday treats. My grandmother made her desserts from scratch. Hope you all enjoy these black-bottom cupcakes as much as I do. Makes 2 dozen

Cupcakes

24 crimped baking cups (foil or paper)

$1\frac{1}{2}$ cups unbleached, all-purpose flour

1 cup sugar

$\frac{1}{4}$ cup unsweetened cocoa powder

1 teaspoon baking soda

$\frac{1}{2}$ teaspoon salt

$\frac{1}{3}$ cup vegetable oil

1 tablespoon white vinegar

1 teaspoon vanilla

Filling

1 (8-ounce) package cream cheese

$\frac{1}{3}$ cup sugar

1 large egg

Pinch salt

1 (6-ounce) package semisweet chocolate chips

1. Preheat the oven to 350°F. Line two 12-cup muffin tins with the baking cups.

2. **To make the cupcakes:** Whisk together the flour, sugar, cocoa, baking soda, and salt in a large mixing bowl. Add 1 cup of water, the oil, vinegar, and vanilla and stir to blend. Spoon the batter into the muffin cups.

3. **To make the filling:** Place the cream cheese and sugar in a medium bowl. Using electric beaters, beat the ingredients until creamy and smooth. Add the egg and salt and beat to mix. Stir in the chocolate chips. Drop an even portion of the filling onto the center of the chocolate batter in each muffin cup. Bake the cupcakes for 15 minutes, or until the cream cheese mixture is pale brown and a wooden skewer inserted into the center of one cupcake comes out clean. Let the cupcakes cool in their tins for several minutes before transferring to wire racks to cool completely.

Richie McDonald

RICHIE MCDONALD was born and raised in Lubbock, Texas. He began singing and writing music while in high school. After meeting Dean Sams at an Opryland USA audition in Arlington, Texas, and again in Nashville shortly thereafter, the group Lonestar was born. Richie has written numerous hits such as "Mr. Mom" and "I'm Already There." His recognizable vocal sound continues to make Lonestar one of country music's favorite groups. Richie and his wife, Lorie, reside outside of Nashville with their three children, Rhett, Mollie, and Maisie.

Richie McDonald with his wife, Lorie, and their children, Rhett, Mollie, and Maisie

I'M ON THE ROAD touring and writing so much with my fellow Lonestar family that time spent at home with my wife, Lorie, and our children—Rhett, Mollie, and Maisie—are treasured moments. We have worked to make our home a great place to spend those times. As a kid, Christmas was always a real special time for me and now as a parent, it means even more. There's nothing greater than seeing the expressions on your kids' faces come Christmas morning.

Lorie and I have created several traditions with our children—hanging up stockings, decorating the house—and as they get older, we're really able to enjoy those moments more. It's something we look forward to all year. I write a lot of songs about my family, and it's times like these that inspire me the most.

Being out on the road, it's hard sometimes to eat healthy, but I really try. Well, when Christmastime comes, that gets put on the back burner—next to all the other great food cooking in our house! Nothing beats Lorie's punch bowl cake though. The kids and I really love it. We never worry about leftovers. Her cake is a big hit.

Merry Christmas to all of you. I hope you enjoy and treasure those special holiday moments with your family this year, and every year to follow.

Already There Punch Bowl Cake

Holidays are busy times, but you can count me there when the punch bowl cake is brought to the table. It's one cake I don't wanna miss. You'll be glad you're there too when you take a bite of this festive treat. Serves 12

1 (8.25-ounce) package yellow cake mix

3 cups milk

2 (3.4-ounce) boxes instant vanilla pudding
   and pie filling mix

1 (10½-ounce) can cherry pie filling

1 (22-ounce) can pineapple chunks, drained

4 medium bananas, peeled and thinly sliced

2 (16-ounce) containers whipped topping,
   such as Cool Whip

1 cup chopped nuts, such as walnuts

1 cup sweetened shredded coconut

1 (6-ounce jar) maraschino cherries, drained

1. Preheat the oven to 350°F. Grease two 8-inch round baking pans.

2. Prepare the cake according to the package directions. Stir well to blend and pour into the prepared baking pans. Bake for 33 to 36 minutes, or until a wooden skewer inserted into the center of one of the cakes comes out clean. Let the cakes cool in the pans for several minutes before turning out onto wire racks to cool completely.

3. Place the milk in a large bowl. Whisk in the pudding mix and continue whisking until thickened.

4. Crumble one of the cakes into a punch bowl, or another very large decorative bowl. Spoon half of the cherry pie filling over the crumbled cake and gently spread half of the prepared vanilla pudding over the cherry filling. Arrange half of the pineapple chunks and banana slices over the vanilla pudding. Gently spread one container of the whipped topping over the fruit. Repeat the process with the remaining cake—crumbled into bits—cherry pie filling, vanilla pudding, pineapple chunks, banana slices, and container of whipped topping. Garnish with the nuts, coconut, and maraschino cherries. Cover the bowl with plastic wrap and chill in the refrigerator for several hours, or until the layers have come together to create a thick puddinglike cake.

Anne Murray

FOR OVER THIRTY YEARS, Canadian-born Anne Murray's unique voice and heartwarming style have made her a household name. Exploding on the scene in 1970 with a song called "Snowbird," Anne received the first American gold record ever awarded to a Canadian female soloist. Having since sold close to fifty million albums, she continues to be one of the top international recording stars.

I WAS RAISED with five brothers and it seemed like our house was bedlam all the time. Christmas was no exception. Mom and Dad did manage to settle things down on Christmas Eve, and we would all sing Christmas songs while my dad picked out the notes with one finger on the piano. We would then go to church and attend midnight mass. Afterward we would go home and eat partridge, a small bird that is a delicacy. My dad was a hunter and we all enjoyed the deer, rabbit, and partridge that he brought home.

After eating, all of us children would drag our tired bodies to bed about 2 A.M. Christmas morning. Mom would then start pulling our Christmas presents out of the attic, where she had hidden them. I think she wore us out on purpose, so we wouldn't hear her getting the gifts out of the attic. She hid things pretty good up there for Christmas, and we were not allowed to go up and snoop around. My brother Harold said he didn't get his bow and arrow set one Christmas because Mom lost it up in the attic, and it is still there to this day. It's a running joke with all my siblings.

Christmas morning was just a great big party of ripping open presents and eating the candy that filled our Christmas stockings. My favorite sweets were Smarties. My family would eat so many sweets, especially Mom, that breakfast was never mentioned. My childhood memories of holiday seasons past are a treasure in my heart and mind.

The last five years I have had so much fun doing a Christmas tour. The audiences are in a festive mood, and I really enjoy sharing the spirit of Christmas with them. I always make it home for Christmas Eve, though. Home is north of Toronto, where my two children were raised. Since I have been on the road the past five years, my daughter now decorates the Christmas tree and helps decorate the house. We sit down as a family on Christmas Eve and watch movies like *It's a Wonderful Life*, *A Christmas Carol*, and *Miracle on 34th Street*.

On Christmas morning, we open our presents and call my mother. For twenty-five years we have been enjoying the cherry cake that she sends to us each Christmas. It is so good. I've never tried to bake one because she always sends us one and it is always perfect. My contribution to our evening Christmas dinner is the turkey with stuffing and all the trimmings. The most important fact about Christmas is that we are together. We laugh and enjoy each other. My son plays the piano and my daughter plays the guitar, so there is always music at our home on the holidays. One of our favorite songs to sing is "O Holy Night."

I want to remind everyone to relax, have fun, and don't take yourself too seriously. Above all, enjoy yourself this holiday season. I certainly will!

Snowbird Cherry Cake

Christmas for this Canadian wouldn't be complete without the much-anticipated cherry cake from Mom—delivered by mail to Toronto every Christmas for twenty-five years running!

Makes 1 Bundt cake

3/4 pound (3 sticks) unsalted butter, softened

2 cups sugar

4 large eggs

1 teaspoon vanilla extract

1 teaspoon almond extract

1 teaspoon lemon extract

4 cups unbleached, all-purpose flour

2 teaspoons baking powder

1 teaspoon salt

1 cup milk

1½ cups halved red candied cherries

1½ cups halved green candied cherries

1. Preheat the oven to 325°F. Grease and flour a 10-inch Bundt pan.

2. Combine the butter and sugar in a large bowl. Using electric beaters, beat the ingredients until creamy and smooth. Beat in the eggs, one at a time, followed by the vanilla, almond, and lemon extracts.

3. Whisk together the flour, baking powder, and salt in a medium bowl. Add half of the flour mixture to the butter mixture, along with ½ cup of the milk. Beat until blended. Repeat the process with the remaining flour mixture and ½ cup of milk. Stir the red and green cherries into the batter and pour into the prepared pan. Bake the cake for 1 hour and 45 minutes, or until a wooden skewer inserted into the cake comes out clean. Let cool in the pan for several minutes before inverting onto a wire rack to cool completely.

Anne Murray with her mother, Marion

Judy Spencer Nelon

JUDY SPENCER NELON began singing at a young age with her two sisters, Linda and Sharon. For a time they toured with Merle Haggard, opening his show with gospel music. Judy is a historian of gospel music and a noted co-author of *This Is My Story,* published by Thomas Nelson Publishing Company. She is vice president of Manna Music, which owns such copyrights as "Come on Ring Those Bells," "How Great Thou Art," "Sweet Spirit," "His Name Is Wonderful," and "Alleluia." She is the first female president of the Southern Gospel Music Guild. She also directs her late husband's music publishing company, Rex Nelon Music. She is passionate about preserving the legacy of gospel music.

IT'S PROBABLY SAFE TO SAY that the Waffle House isn't on the list of America's most romantic places, but that Southern restaurant will always hold a special memory for me. It had been a long time since there had been any romance in my life when Bill and Gloria Gaither and some of the Homecoming Friends decided to do a little match-making. They began working on fixing me up with a strikingly handsome and talented widower, Rex Nelon. We hit it off great, but of all the things we had in common, a hometown wasn't one of them. Rex lived in Atlanta, Georgia, and I lived in Nashville, Tennessee. But thanks to cell phones and all the Homecoming events, our long-distance relationship was going so well by Christmas that Rex said he would enjoy having me join him for the holiday in Asheville, North Carolina, at the old Nelon family home place. He said his mom, then eighty-nine years of age, would be making all his favorite holiday foods, including her signature pound cake, as she did every Christmas.

Of course I said yes.

The dinner was every bit as good as Rex had promised, and later that evening Rex and I exchanged gifts and cards. He gave me his card to open first, but as soon as I saw it I recognized it as

Judy Spencer Nelon with her husband, Rex

the exact same card that I had picked out for him! It said "Only You." Obviously, we were on the same wavelength!

But after the holiday festivities, as Rex was driving me back to my home in Tennessee, we stopped at a Waffle House in Knoxville for dinner.

Right there in that smoky Waffle House, Rex leaned across the table, took both of my hands in his, and tenderly looked into my eyes and asked me to marry him!

Of course I said yes!

I will always be grateful for the wonderful Christmas gift God gave me that night. Even though our time together was short, we lived it with zest. I realize even without Rex I can still ring those Christmas bells with family because of God's promise and His amazing grace.

Ring Those Bells Pound Cake

This wonderful dessert was handed down by the family of my late husband, Rex Nelon. It will make you want to sing, "Come on Ring Those Bells."
Makes 2 large loaves

Cake

12 large eggs
1 pound (4 sticks) unsalted butter, softened
1 pound sugar (2 cups)
1 pound unbleached, all-purpose flour
   (3 cups sifted)
1 teaspoon baking powder

Icing

1$\frac{1}{2}$ cups confectioner's sugar
2 tablespoons milk
1$\frac{1}{2}$ teaspoons unsalted butter
$\frac{1}{2}$ teaspoon vanilla extract

1. Preheat the oven to 325°F. Grease two 9-inch loaf pans.

2. **To make the cake:** Separate the eggs, placing the yolks in a medium bowl and the whites in a large bowl. Set aside.

3. Combine the butter and sugar in a large bowl. Blend until creamy and smooth. Add the egg yolks and stir until mixed. Gradually add the flour, stirring well after each addition.

4. Add the baking powder to the egg whites and with electric beaters, beat the whites until they form soft peaks. Stir one third of the beaten egg whites into the yolk mixture to lighten it. Using a rubber spatula, gently fold in the remaining whites. Spoon the batter into the prepared loaf pans. Bake the loaves for 1$\frac{1}{4}$ to 1$\frac{1}{2}$ hours, or until a wooden skewer inserted into the center of one loaf comes out clean. Let the pound cakes cool in their pans for several minutes before inverting onto wire racks to cool completely.

5. **To make the icing:** Place the confectioner's sugar in a large bowl. Place the milk and butter in a small microwave-proof bowl and heat on high until the butter has melted, about 12 seconds. Add to the confectioner's sugar along with the vanilla, and blend until the icing is creamy and smooth. Spread over the top of each cooled pound cake.

Buck Owens

BUCK OWENS, perhaps best known as co-host of *Hee Haw*, a long-running country comedy show, is an icon in every sense. In addition to his enormous success with *Hee Haw*, he has enjoyed a string of number one hits that has made him one of the most durable country entertainers in history and a Country Music Hall of Fame inductee. As a songwriter, he has penned numerous internationally known standards. As a businessman, he has demonstrated his flair for making great decisions.

Buck Owens with his granddaughter, Jennifer

IT WAS 1940 and we had moved to the outskirts of a little town called Mesa, in Arizona. Up until that time we had always lived eight to twelve miles outside of the nearest town. There in Mesa was the first place we'd ever had electricity and an indoor toilet. Our first Christmas in Mesa was incredible. We got our first Christmas tree. I had seen a few Christmas trees, but they were always at someone else's house.

My uncle Vernon and aunt Lucille lived in a trailer house behind us. Uncle Vernon played the guitar, and occasionally he'd have some of his musician friends congregate at our house.

One of the fellows who came over one day brought a mandolin, and I absolutely fell in love with the sound. My uncle kept one he had borrowed hanging on his wall. When I'd get home from school, no one was around but us kids, so I would go out to my uncle's trailer house, take that mandolin off the wall, slip inside an old barn, and pick and pick as long as I dared. I was certain this was a punishable offense, but I couldn't help myself and just avoided getting caught. Music became so exciting to me that I tried to listen and watch it being performed whenever possible.

That Christmas, my folks actually bought me my own mandolin! It wasn't a new one, but I didn't care. Actually, I couldn't believe it—how did they know? Well, so much for my secret after-school passion! I remember that I slept with that mandolin for two weeks; I just couldn't put it down. The first song I tried to figure out was called "Just Because." I remember my mother calling out through the wall, "Who is playin' that?" I replied, "I am, Mother, I am." She said, "That's real good, son, now put down the mandolin and go to sleep!"

Note: Our friend Buck Owens passed away on March 25, 2006. We will miss him.

Mother Owens's Banana Pudding

This is one of my all-time favorites. When I was growing up in Texas, Mother would fix up big batches of this for all us kids. We liked it so much, that somehow what leftovers there were never did stay in the icebox too long. Whenever she fixed it for me, I got very greedy with it and sometimes I just refused to share with anyone. Mother cooked with "dabs," "fingerfuls," and "just a bit's," so these amounts are as close as anybody can come to a recipe. I hope you enjoy it as much as my family does. Serves 6

1 cup sugar
3 tablespoons unbleached, all-purpose flour
$\frac{1}{2}$ teaspoon salt
$2\frac{1}{2}$ cups milk
2 large eggs
1 (8-ounce) container whipped topping, such as Cool Whip
1 (12-ounce) box vanilla wafers
4 large bananas, peeled and thinly sliced

1. Whisk together the sugar, flour, and salt in a large saucepan. Whisk in the milk until well blended. Whisk in the eggs, turn the heat to medium, and whisk the mixture until thickened. Let cool. Using a rubber spatula, gently fold in the whipped topping until incorporated.

2. Line the bottom of an 8-inch square baking dish with half of the vanilla wafers. Cover the wafers with half of the banana slices. Spoon half of the pudding over the bananas. Repeat this process, ending with the pudding. Cover the dish with plastic wrap and chill in the refrigerator for several hours, or until the layers have come together to create a thick puddinglike cake.

Dolly Parton

BORN ON JANUARY 19, 1946, in Locust Ridge, Tennessee, into a poor family that would eventually include twelve children, Dolly Parton learned early to escape the hardships of life through her vivid and far-ranging imagination. She would make up songs, even before she could read and write. Moving to Nashville after graduating high school in 1954, Dolly struggled for a number of years until she had her first hit, "Dumb Blonde," on Monument Records in 1967. From there, she began accumulating countless successes. Superstar, singer, songwriter, actress, and businesswoman, Dolly continues to be everyone's favorite. And how many other people have a theme park named after them?

MY MOST MEMORABLE Christmas was the one for which I personally received the least. When Mama and Daddy married, he was only seventeen and she was fifteen. They truly loved each other, but they were both poor. Daddy had never even been able to give Mama a wedding ring. One Christmas he gathered us all together and explained to those of us who were old enough to understand that there wouldn't be the usual store-bought gifts we had come to expect over the years. Daddy had used this year's money to buy Mama a ring! There was, however, one gift for the person who could find the ring where Daddy had hidden it. This set off a frenzy of searching for the ring. I looked every place that could accommodate a ring. Of course, all of this was accompanied by wild guesses as to what the one gift might be and confident proclamations of what each searcher would do with the gift once he or she had won it.

We searched high and low until the ring was found! Months before, we had finally gotten electricity, so it was the first Christmas that a string of garish bubble lights was added to our tree, ensuring our unending fascination. The ring was found around one of those bubbling glass tubes and immediately rushed to Mama. Everybody shared Daddy's pride as she slipped it on her left-hand finger. A chorus of very genuine "oohs" and "ahhs" went up. The "one gift," as it turned out, was a big box of chocolates that we could all share. That was Daddy's way. Those chocolates were so sweet they could make your teeth hurt, but still not as sweet as the memories of that Christmas.

Dolly's Jolly Cheesecake Pudding

Memories of Christmas are made even sweeter when you share my cheesecake pudding with family and friends. It's a great dessert for entertaining. Grab a spoon and a bowl and start in on the sweetest taste this side of the Smoky Mountains.
Serves 6 to 8

Crust

1 cup unbleached, all-purpose flour
8 tablespoons (1 stick) unsalted butter, softened
1/2 cup pecan or walnut pieces

Filling

1 (8-ounce) package cream cheese
1 cup sugar
1 (8-ounce) container whipped topping, such as Cool Whip
3 cups milk
2 (3.9-ounce) boxes instant chocolate pudding and pie filling mix

1. Preheat the oven to 350°F.

2. **To make the crust:** Place the flour and butter in a medium bowl. Stir well to blend. Mix in the nuts. Press the mixture in an even layer across the bottom of a 13 by 9-inch baking dish. Bake for 15 minutes, or until golden. Let cool on a wire rack.

3. **To make the filling:** Combine the cream cheese and sugar in a medium bowl. Beat until creamy and smooth. Using a rubber spatula, gently fold in the whipped topping until incorporated. Gently spread over the cooled crust.

4. Place the milk in a large bowl. Whisk in the pudding mix and continue whisking until the pudding has thickened. Gently spread the pudding over the cream cheese layer. Chill the cheesecake pudding in the refrigerator until ready to serve.

Andy Griggs

RAISED IN WEST MONROE, Louisiana, Andy Griggs was exposed to country music at an early age by his guitar-playing father. Andy was just ten when his dad died of cancer; he remembers listening to his father's favorite Merle Haggard album as a way to help deal with the grief. Andy faced tragedy again at age eighteen when his brother Mason, a songwriter and musician, died of a heart attack. In mourning, Andy picked up his brother's guitar and began to play—it made him feel close to his brother. Soon he couldn't put the guitar down.

With some vague sense of making music for a living, Andy wandered into Nashville in 1994 with no demo tape, no contacts, nothing. All he had was his voice and the desire to use it. He got the opportunity to audition live for Joe Galante at RCA Records two years later. Instead of the love ballad that was expected, Andy tore into Hank Williams Jr.'s harrowing "In the Arms of Cocaine." It was that edgy "rebel" gesture that set Andy apart and launched his career.

Andy has already achieved nine hits in the top ten, two of which went to number one. He is a real family man with a heart for others, and a passion for his music.

THE BIGGEST CHRISTMAS memory I have is of the family gathering around the fire every Christmas Eve to pray and sing. Another tradition Mama started, and that we are carrying on with the girls, is to hang a new handmade ornament every year.

When I was four or five years old, my uncle Connie, bless his heart, dressed up as Santa Claus for the Christmas party at church. Nobody knew it was him, but when I sat on Santa's lap, there were tobacco stains all the way down his cotton beard. The whole time I'm thinking, did Santa Claus really chew that much tobacco? I mean it was just a river of tobacco stains. And the way he laughed, I knew it must be Uncle Connie. My brother and I figured it out that night, that either Santa Claus was Uncle Connie or there was no Santa Claus at all. My favorite Christmas song is "Santa Looked a Lot Like Daddy." That's made me smile the most.

As an adult, my greatest Christmastime has been this last year. I have the love of my life and her two daughters, who are like my own. This is the first time in my life that I've ever looked at a Christmas tree and gifts from a father's standpoint, wanting to spoil these little girls. I figured if I ever had a kid, I'd be buying pop guns and coonskin caps, but I'm buying talking Barbie dolls and kittens that meow. It's a wonderful feeling.

Heavenly Coconut Cake and Coconut Frosting

Growing up in church I always looked forward to the fellowships because there would be lots of good food, including at least one tasty coconut cake. The problem was everyone wanted a piece of that cake. You had to grab a piece quick or you'd be left with crumbs. Now I buy a little coconut-cake insurance and bake one myself for Christmas! **Makes 1 Bundt cake**

Cake

1½ pounds (6 sticks) unsalted butter, softened

3 cups sugar

5 large eggs

2 teaspoons coconut extract

1 teaspoon vanilla extract

3 cups unbleached, all-purpose flour

1 teaspoon baking powder

1 teaspoon salt

¾ cup unsweetened coconut milk

Frosting

1½ cups sugar

1 tablespoon light corn syrup

Pinch salt

2 large egg whites

1 teaspoon coconut extract

½ teaspoon vanilla extract

1 (7-ounce) package sweetened, shredded coconut

1. Preheat the oven to 325°F. Grease and flour a 10-inch Bundt pan.

2. To make the cake: Combine the butter and sugar in a large bowl. Using electric beaters, beat the ingredients until creamy and smooth. Beat in the eggs, one at a time, followed by the extracts.

3. Whisk together the flour, baking powder, and salt in a medium bowl. Add half of the flour mixture to the shortening mixture, along with 2 tablespoons of water and half of the coconut milk. Beat until blended. Repeat the process with the remaining flour mixture, 2 tablespoons of water, and the remaining coconut milk. Pour into the prepared Bundt pan and bake for 70 minutes, or until a wooden skewer inserted into the cake comes out clean. Let cool in the pan for several minutes before inverting onto a wire rack to cool completely.

4. To make the frosting: Bring water to a simmer in the bottom of a double boiler. Meanwhile, blend together the sugar, corn syrup, salt, and ⅓ cup of water in the top insert of the double boiler off the heat. Place the egg whites in a medium bowl and with electric beaters whip until they form soft peaks. Add to the sugar mixture and, with electric beaters, beat the mixture for 1 minute.

5. Place the insert over the simmering water in the bottom of the double boiler over medium heat. With the electric beaters on high, beat the frosting for 7 minutes. Beat in the coconut and vanilla extracts and remove the double boiler insert from the heat. The frosting should be white, shiny, and fluffy.

6. Place the Bundt cake, rounded side up, on a decorative plate and spread with the frosting. Sprinkle the shredded coconut over the cake.

Andy Griggs with his wife, Renee, and their children, Savannah and Amara

T.G. Sheppard

*I*N 1965, Bill Browder got into the record promotion business. In a short time, he was successful. Then in 1972, he heard a song that changed his life forever; it was Bobby David's composition "Devil in the Bottle." After being turned down by eight record labels, he cut the song himself. He changed his name to T.G. Sheppard and made a deal with Motown Records. He followed "Devil in the Bottle" with hits like "When Can We Do This Again" and "Trying to Beat the Morning Home." In 1976, T.G. signed with Warner Brothers Records. There he had a string of ten number-one hits, including "Last Cheater's Waltz," "Only One You," "Party Time," and "I Loved 'Em Everyone." T.G. is still touring.

CHRISTMAS HAS BEEN a mixed blessing to me. It has brought much joy and some sadness. My most memorable Christmas was in 1991. I was at my father's house in Humboldt, Tennessee, when he passed away on Christmas Eve.

My father had suffered for years with cancer. I had watched his painful existence and prayed on many occasions for his release from the dreadful disease. That night, God in His infinite wisdom relieved my father of his suffering. Although I will miss him forever, it was a great relief to know my father was finally at peace.

On a happier note, Christmas at Graceland with Elvis was always a delight—he was such a giving person, especially to his friends and employees. Elvis and I had been good friends from my days at RCA. I remember one Christmas in particular. We were all gathered inside Graceland (I remember there were lots of ladies), and all the employees were asked to go outside. In the driveway, there were numerous new automobiles. Each person was given a key and told to find the car the key would fit. Making the gift even more special, inside the trunk of each and every car was a fur coat for the wife or girlfriend. You can imagine the delight of everyone.

Elvis always loved Christmas, and Graceland was so beautifully decorated. It made you have a warm feeling inside just looking at it. As much as the beauty of Graceland would lift you up, Elvis would lift you higher. The joy of Christmas, of love, and of giving would radiate from his persona. He was always a kid at heart, but the spirit of Christmas brought that out of Elvis even more.

Every day spent with Elvis was special, but during Christmas it was even more so. To me it was a time of family, close friends, and being with someone bigger than life. Thank you, Elvis.

Feel Good All Over Bread Pudding

Christmastime has brought both cheer and tears for me, but no matter what the mood has been, this bread pudding has always seemed to brighten up the holidays. This dessert continues to be one of the favorites I look forward to every year.
Serves 8

Pudding

4 cups crumbled biscuits or cubes of fresh white
   bread
2 cups low-fat milk
4 large eggs
$^3/_4$ cup sugar
3 tablespoons unsalted butter or margarine
1 teaspoon vanilla extract
$^3/_4$ cup raisins

Lemon Sauce

$^2/_3$ cup sweetened condensed milk
1 teaspoon grated lemon zest
$^1/_4$ cup lemon juice
4 large egg yolks

1. Preheat the oven to 325°F. Grease a 13 by 9-inch baking dish.

2. **To make the pudding:** Scatter the crumbled biscuits over the bottom of the prepared dish. Pour the milk over the biscuits and let stand for 10 minutes for the milk to be absorbed.

3. Whisk together the eggs with the sugar. Melt the butter in a small saucepan over medium heat. Add to the egg mixture, along with the vanilla and raisins. Pour over the saturated biscuits and gently stir the mixture to blend. Bake for 45 to 50 minutes or until the custard has set. Let cool slightly.

4. **To make the lemon sauce:** Whisk together the condensed milk, lemon zest, and lemon juice in a small saucepan. Whisk in the egg yolks and cook over low heat, whisking constantly, until the sauce has thickened. Spoon the warm lemon sauce over each portion of bread pudding.

Kenny Chesney with T.G. Sheppard

Pam Tillis

*P*AM TILLIS, daughter of the famous songwriter and singer Mel Tillis, has been outstanding as a singer, a songwriter, and an actress. As a recording artist, she has had six number-one and seventeen top-ten hits, in addition to a Grammy award and two Country Music Association awards, including Female Vocalist of the Year. In the new millennium, Pam was inducted into the *Grand Ole Opry* and starred on Broadway to rave reviews in the musical *Smokey Joe's Café.*

IN THE TILLIS HOUSEHOLD for quite a few years now, Christmastime has been a time to team up, entertain, and spread some of our particular brand of zany cheer. I've done several solo Christmas tours, but I really love the Christmas shows I've done with my family the most. It's a lot of work, but so rewarding.

Every time I'm on stage with my brother and sister, I can't help but reflect on how this all started in Mom and Dad's living room singing into hairbrushes, paper towel rolls, or whatever kind of "microphones" we could find.

My favorite memories are of Carrie, Connie, and me singing Andrews Sisters' harmony to Dad's "b-b-b-b"-ing on "Jingle Bells"; standing in the wings watching baby sis, Carrie, wow the crowd with "Ave Maria"; and teaching all the nieces and nephews to entertain (of course, they always stole the show because they were just so darn cute). Add to these favorite memories all six feet three inches of my brother Sonny in a bright green elf suit, my nephew Marshall struggling to keep up his saggy elf tights while the audience is laughing so hard they're crying (not to mention the family hysterically laughing in the wings), and Daddy's warm beautiful tenor on "Let There Be Peace on Earth" while the snow came down from the ceiling.

These aren't home-around-the-fireplace memories. We have plenty of those, too, but for a member of a family with show business in their blood, these are some of my very favorite, very musical memories.

Shake-the-Sugar-Tree Raspberry Linzertorte

Being on the road, entertaining during the holidays creates unique memories. This raspberry linzertorte, a favorite of mine, always makes me feel a little closer to home, no matter what city I am performing in or what stage I am standing on.
Serves 8 to 10

> 1½ cups unbleached, all-purpose flour
> ⅔ cup firmly packed light brown sugar
> ½ cup finely ground almonds
> ½ teaspoon baking powder
> ½ teaspoon ground cinnamon
> ½ teaspoon salt
> 8 tablespoons (1 stick) unsalted butter, softened
> 1 large egg
> 1¼ cups seedless raspberry jam

1. Whisk together the flour, sugar, almonds, baking powder, cinnamon, and salt in a large bowl. Beat in the butter and egg until the mixture forms a soft dough. Set aside one third of the dough (to make the lattice) in a small bowl.

2. Lay out a large piece of parchment paper and place the rest of the dough in the center. Roll out the dough to create a circle large enough to press across the bottom and up the sides of a 10-inch fluted tart pan with a removable bottom. Gently press the crust into the tart pan.

3. To make the lattice, roll out the reserved portion of dough so that it forms a $1/2$-inch-thick rectangle, approximately 5 inches wide and 10 inches long. Cut the rectangle into ten $1/2$-inch-wide strips. Place the strips on a parchment-lined baking sheet and chill them and the crust in the refrigerator for 30 minutes.

4. While the crust and lattice strips chill, heat the raspberry jam in a small saucepan over medium heat until melted. Stir and let cool slightly.

5. Preheat the oven to 350°F.

6. Remove the crust and strips from the refrigerator. Pour the raspberry jam into the crust. Weave the strips over the crust so that they form a lattice pattern. Trim off any excess dough and press it along the edges of the tart pan. Bake the linzertorte for 30 to 35 minutes or until the pastry is golden. Remove from the oven—the jam will be quite liquidy—and let the linzertorte cool on a wire rack until the pastry has reached room temperature and the jam has thickened.

Tanya Tucker

ANYA TUCKER's family had no idea she could sing until one day as a small child she asked her father, Beau Tucker, if he would like to hear her sing a song. "Sweetheart, you couldn't sing your way out of a paper sack," he replied. That was Daddy's mistake. Over the next thirty-odd years, Tanya has enjoyed one of the most successful careers in music. Starting with the song "Delta Dawn" at the age of thirteen, Tanya collected a list of hits that led to Female Vocalist of the Year honors at the 1991 Country Music Association's awards show. Unlike most teen sensations, Tanya is still a force to be reckoned with.

Tanya Tucker with her children, Grayson, Layla, and Presley

WE HAD OUR GREATEST Christmas ever just last year. Some of our close friends were near Steamboat, Colorado, when I had a show. We decided to stay together in a friend's beautiful home in the mountains. We loved the breathtaking view and felt as if we were in a wonderful winter wonderland for our Christmas holiday.

So the kids would feel a touch of home in Steamboat, I had eight boxes of Christmas ornaments shipped in from Nashville, and we cut down a live tree. Boy was it ugly, but we all still had a lot of fun putting our own decorations on it.

My children, Presley, Grayson, and Layla, all love to ski as much as I do. We couldn't wait to hit the snowy Colorado slopes. I stood Layla between my legs so I could help guide her down the slopes. The other kids saw us and began laughing. We all got so tickled that we started to fall; and instead of skiing down, we ended up rolling to the bottom of the slope. We tossed and giggled with each other in the powdery white snow for a while. What a great Christmas memory for all of us.

Then it was time for something hot to drink so we gathered ourselves up and headed for our holiday home in the mountains. It was a special time, snuggling up together and sipping on hot mugs of cocoa with marshmallows while we sang "Jingle Bells." The kids love to sing Christmas carols. After all, their Mama is a rock-and-roll gal.

Mama's Delta Dawn Holiday Special

Two of the traditions I remember most at home during the holidays were that my mom and dad always would give me one large present and would always prepare this special holiday dessert. One Christmas, they even gave me a brand-new car. Did I think I was special or what? I always include this dish with our Christmas meal and at special times throughout the year. It takes me back to my childhood. Serves 8

5 navel oranges

5 sweet-tart apples

5 large bananas

1 fresh pineapple

2 (15-ounce) cans fruit cocktail, drained

2 (7½-ounce) cans mandarin oranges, drained

2 cups pecan halves

4 cups (2 pints) whipping cream

¼ cup sugar

1. Peel the oranges and with a very sharp knife, slice off the pith and skin. Cut out each section, so that you have a wedge of fruit without any pith or skin. Transfer the wedges to a large decorative bowl. Peel, core, and dice each apple and add to the oranges. Peel each banana and cut into small chunks. Remove the outer skin from the pineapple, core the fruit, and cut into small pieces. Add to the fruit bowl, along with the fruit cocktail, mandarin oranges, and pecans.

2. Place the cream in a large bowl. With electric beaters, whip until soft peaks form. Gradually beat in the sugar. Using a rubber spatula, gently fold the whipped cream into the fruit and nut mixture. Chill the dessert in the refrigerator until ready to serve.

Josh Turner

MCA ARTIST JOSH TURNER made a huge impression with his first single "Long Black Train," a traditional-sounding country gospel song, which he wrote while a student at Nashville's Belmont University. The inspiration to write the song came to him after listening to the entire Hank Williams Sr. box set in the school's library. His deep baritone voice and singing style place him in the category of such greats as Waylon Jennings and Johnny Cash. Not a bad place to be.

Josh Turner with his wife, Jennifer

MY FONDEST MEMORIES are of South Carolina summers—swimming at Grandmama's pool, playing Wiffle ball in the backyard with my siblings, and eating blueberries all summer long. These were, and still are, my favorite fruit. Our family had about seven or eight blueberry bushes and my grandparents had about forty or fifty! My mama would freeze and can the berries in the summer so we could have jams and desserts all year long. My very favorite cobbler in the world is blueberry. Mama used a recipe she inherited from her grandmother, Granny Weaver. I never really got to know Granny Weaver but we sure feel her presence when we are making up batches of blueberry cobbler, especially at Christmastime.

I purchased my first home last fall, and yes, you guessed it, my wife, Jennifer, and I planted blueberry bushes to remind us of our childhoods in South Carolina. The family tradition of picking blueberries in our own yard and using them for the delicious Granny Weaver blueberry cobbler will allow us to enjoy Christmas scents from seasons past.

Granny Weaver's Choo-Choo Blueberry Cobbler

When Granny Weaver's blueberry cobbler is brought to the holiday dinner table, everyone arrives on time. It's too good to miss, so choo-choo on over to the desserts. Serves 6

4 tablespoons ($\frac{1}{2}$ stick) unsalted butter
1 cup unbleached, all-purpose flour
$\frac{3}{4}$ cup sugar
$1\frac{1}{2}$ teaspoons baking powder
$\frac{1}{2}$ teaspoon salt
$\frac{3}{4}$ cup milk
2 cups fresh or frozen blueberries

1. Preheat the oven to 350°F.

2. Melt the butter in a small saucepan over medium heat. Pour into a $1\frac{1}{2}$-quart baking dish.

3. Whisk together the flour, $\frac{1}{4}$ cup of the sugar, the baking powder, and salt in a medium bowl. Add the milk and stir well to blend. Pour into the buttered baking dish.

4. Place the remaining $\frac{1}{2}$ cup of sugar in a medium bowl. Add $\frac{1}{3}$ cup of water and stir until the sugar has dissolved. Stir in the blueberries. Pour this mixture over the batter, but do not mix. Bake for 40 to 45 minutes, or until the batter has puffed around the blueberries and turned golden. Let the cobbler rest for 10 minutes before serving.

Rhonda Vincent

RHONDA VINCENT is a modern-day bluegrass singer. Her contemporary sound with progressive chord structures and multirange, fast-paced vocals have set her apart from traditional bluegrass musicians. Her black leather jeans, her flawless style of mandolin playing, and her original music have created a modern version of the great bluegrass performers of the past. In 2001, she was named International Bluegrass Association Entertainer of the Year. For four years she was named Female Vocalist of the Year and in 2004 was a Grammy winner. The *Wall Street Journal* has called her the "queen of bluegrass."

CHRISTMAS WAS ALWAYS a wonderful time growing up, and continues to be one of my favorite times of the year. It is my mother's favorite holiday, and she always made Christmas extra special. And it wasn't in just one or two ways. Christmas was a yearlong project. She saved her special "Christmas money" all year by faithfully making her weekly contributions to her Christmas Club Account at the Commerce Bank.

Thanksgiving marked the official beginning of our Christmas celebration preparations. One of our special traditions was the annual Christmas program that we would put on the Sunday night before Christmas. Each child was given a verse to memorize and recite for the program. For weeks, I worked hard to remember each word. I was never quite sure I would ever remember my assigned verse. But somehow, each year when it was time to step to the microphone—butterflies and all—the words managed to come out just right.

I will never forget one very special Christmas. All the usual traditions were honored, but the night after Christmas brought a strange excitement in the air, almost like Christmas Eve all over again. My dad sent me to Grandma Erma's house to stay overnight but didn't tell me why. The next day I found out. On December 27, Dad called to

say that I had a new baby brother! He said he had a real set of lungs and then held the phone so I could hear him screaming from the hospital nursery down the hallway. Wow, he was born in December, just like Jesus. What an extraspecial Christmas!

Grandma's Classic Caramel Dumplings

Christmas at Grandma's house is all about eating her Classic Caramel Dumplings. You'll be making them a family tradition too. Serves 8

Garnish

½ cup coarsely chopped pecans

1 tablespoon unsalted butter, melted

½ teaspoon salt

1 cup whipping cream

Sugar to taste

Sauce

4 tablespoons (½ stick) unsalted butter

1 cup firmly packed brown sugar

1 teaspoon vanilla extract

Dumplings

1 cup white self-rising flour
¼ cup sugar
⅓ cup milk
3 tablespoons unsalted butter, melted

1. Preheat the oven to 350°F.

2. **To make the garnish:** Combine the pecans, butter, and salt in a small bowl. Toss to mix and scatter on a baking sheet. Bake, stirring occasionally, for 10 to 12 minutes or until the pecans are lightly roasted. Remove and let cool. (You will whip the cream after the dumplings have baked.)

3. Increase the oven temperature to 400°F.

4. **To make the sauce:** Melt the butter in a 10-inch ovenproof skillet (such as cast iron) over medium heat. Add the sugar and stir until the sugar has melted, about 1 minute. Stir in 1¾ cups of hot water and the vanilla. Bring the mixture to a boil, reduce the heat to low, and let the caramel simmer while you make the dumplings.

5. **To make the dumplings:** Whisk together the flour and sugar in a medium bowl. Stir in the milk and the butter and mix well. Using a large spoon, drop one eighth of the dumpling batter into the hot caramel sauce. Continue making 7 more dumplings in this manner, until there are 8 dumplings sitting in the caramel. Bake the dumplings for 20 to 25 minutes or until they are golden.

6. To serve, place the whipping cream in a medium bowl and whip until soft peaks form. Add sugar to taste and whip again to incorporate. Lay out 8 dessert bowls. Place a dumpling in each bowl and top with some of the caramel sauce. Garnish with a dollop of whipped cream and some roasted pecans.

Rhonda Vincent with her band in Santaland

Photograph Credits

Photograph of Jennings family, page 5, courtesy of Beth Gwinn.

Photograph of Kris Kristofferson and Donnie Fritts, page 6, courtesy of Terry Pace.

Photograph of Brenda Lee, page 9, courtesy of Dennis Carney.

Photograph of Tony Brown, page 16, courtesy of Trey Franjoy.

Photograph of Terre Thomas, page 20, courtesy of John Zacher.

Photograph of Michael Peterson, page 30, courtesy of the U.S. Army.

Photograph of Ronnie Milsap, page 42, courtesy of Jim McGuire.

Photograph of John Michael Montgomery, page 48, courtesy of Lee Thomas Photography.

Photograph of William Lee Golden, page 52, courtesy of Loveless Fine Photography.

Photograph of Jerry Schilling, page 56, courtesy of Jerry Schilling Management.

Photograph of Jett Williams, page 60, courtesy of Jim Shadrick.

Photograph of Alan Jackson, cover and page 64, courtesy of Russ Harrington.

Photograph of Loretta Lynn, cover and page 67, courtesy of Russ Harrington.

Photograph of Vince Gill, page 82, courtesy of Jerene Gill.

Photograph of Bill Anderson, page 86, courtesy of Dennis Carney Photography.

Photograph of Willie Nelson, cover and page 92, courtesy of Heidi Raphael.

Photograph of Charlie Daniels, cover and page 110, courtesy of Dean Tubb.

Photograph of Dan Truman, page 113, courtesy of Russ Harrington.

Photograph of Amy Grant, cover and page 118, courtesy of Andrew Eccles.

Photograph of George Jones, cover and page 121, courtesy of Dennis Carney Photography.

Photograph of Buddy Killen, page 126, courtesy of Melinda Norris Photography.

Photograph of Pam Tillis, cover and page 145, courtesy of the Tillis Family Archives.

Photograph of Tanya Tucker, page 146, courtesy of Patricia Presley Photography.

Country Stars

Recipe Index